# *how to be*
# body
# happy

I ♡ u

Olivia

This book has been produced in collaboration with a
counsellor and a specialist eating disorder dietitian.

First published in Great Britain in 2024 by Wren & Rook

ISBN: 978 1 5263 6689 4

1 3 5 7 9 10 8 6 4 2

MIX
Paper from
responsible sources
FSC® C104740

Wren & Rook
An imprint of
Hachette Children's Group
Part of Hodder & Stoughton
Carmelite House
50 Victoria Embankment
London EC4Y 0DZ

An Hachette UK Company
www.hachette.co.uk
www.hachettechildrens.co.uk

Printed and bound in Great Britain by Clays Ltd, Elcograf S.p.A.

# Olivia Kirkby

## *how to be*
# body
# happy

### feel comfortable
### in your skin

wren
&rook

To my psychiatrist and dietitians who helped me in recovery. I am a small drop in your ocean but for me you made mine and will forever be such a massive role in my story 🫂

And to my followers, I wouldn't have made it this far in recovery without you and neither would these words. I love you 🫶

*Olivia Kirkby*

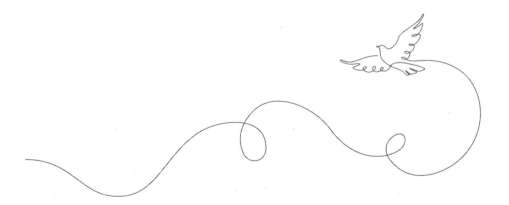

# CONTENTS

# ✦ Introduction ✦

## A note from Olivia

*Hi and welcome :)*

I can't believe I'm actually getting to say this . . . Thank you **SO** much for picking up my book. Right now, you're probably going through a lot of changes. You may be getting your first taste of freedom and independence, going through secondary school and meeting new friends, or maybe even dating.

You might also be discovering more about what really makes you, well, you – experimenting with make-up and fashion trends, or wondering what other people think about how you look and the clothes you wear.

Being a teenager can be so fun and . . . honestly, it can also be really, really hard. You're changing so much; not just the way you feel about certain stuff, but the way you look too. There are things that are new and exciting, and there are things that suck, and then there are things that are, actually, just a bit ***weird.***

Boobs, pubes, periods, spots, the lil dimples on the back of your legs . . . and oh so much more! And just when you think you've got used to the way you look, you notice another bit changing or something else you're not all that comfortable with.

You might have noticed a lil thing called diet culture creeping up everywhere around you, and your friends, your parents or other adults talking about their own bodies or other people's bodies in a negative way and discussing diets or ways to change how you eat. Your friends might have said mean things about their own appearance, talking about the bits of themselves they don't like.

**Maybe you look in the mirror and focus on the things you don't love about yourself too?**

The way we feel about our bodies is a subject that's really very close to my heart; it's something I think about a lot. I think there are a lot of reasons why so many girls struggle with their body image and how they look. Perhaps you feel pressure to look a certain way to fit in with your friends or to look like people you see online. You may worry what other people think about the way you look, such as that person you're crushing on. Or maybe you've had negative comments about your body from someone close to you?

The trouble is that all this pressure can build up, and if you struggle with low self-esteem, you might:

✦ **Hide your body in oversized clothes**

✦ **Stop going out in public because you feel so self-conscious**

✦ **Go on strict diets and perhaps even develop disordered eating**

✦ *And, at the very, very worst, develop an eating disorder*

Growing up wasn't easy for me. I felt ugly and thought I'd be stuck feeling like that forever. I even thought that having to go on diets was what being a woman was all about. Oh boy was I wrong, and although I know that now, I didn't see it back then.

What started as lil worries about not being 'good enough' led me into dieting and trying to change how I looked. So much so that I didn't care about my health and I didn't care about hurting my body. I was just so desperate to feel better about myself. I started to take diet advice from an influencer, which I thought would help me control what I ate, because I would have done anything in order to 'fix' what I believed was wrong with my body. I slowly started to lose myself completely. It was no longer about dieting – it became much more than that. This led me to develop anorexia – an eating disorder and serious mental health condition.

For a while, I was so unwell and miserable, I stopped going out. I stopped seeing my friends. I stopped going out for meals. I just couldn't deal with it, and I didn't want anyone to see me. Thankfully, with medical treatment and lots of support, I gradually got better. I even learned to accept the way I look, including my cute lil squishy bits.

It was a very long journey to recovery for me, but once I was finally feeling happier and more self-confident, I realised that a lot of the stuff I'd seen online had fuelled my insecurity. I'd always been so afraid of letting people see the 'real' me. But, in 2020, rather than hiding away any longer, I decided to set myself free and, hopefully, inspire other girls like me by sharing TikTok videos showing how I actually look, including all the bits I spent years trying to hide.

I even posted videos showing my back rolls and my squishy lil belly! I was nervous, but my posts got a really positive reaction from others. Since then, I'm proud to have built a lil supportive bubble of the internet. And now you're here, reading my book, and I'm sooo happy about that. :))) Filled with my lil tips, this book is going to be your 'go to' guide to feeling better about your body.

**Listen, I'm not an expert on diet and nutrition. I can only tell you about my own journey of feeling unhappy in my skin and how I have learned to accept all the things – like my lil dimples and my lumps and bumps – that I used to hate. I'm so excited to be sharing my experiences to help other girls struggling with their own body image.**

**Thankfully, we also have two amazing professionals here to help: counsellor Mayvrill Freeston-Roberts**

**and specialist eating disorder dietitian Christina de Beukelaar (who is one of the amazing dietitians who helped me in my eating disorder recovery). I can't wait for you to read what they have to say too.**

It hurts my heart to think of anyone else going down the same path that I did, feeling desperately unhappy about their body. I want to show you another way – one where you can see yourself differently and know the importance of being truly healthy (not the restrictive kind, but the one where you actually eat enough and include all the food groups!). You might start to accept or even like the lil things you may have believed to be 'wrong' all along.

The truth is that this is the book I needed when I was growing up. So I hope that every time you read these pages, you feel less alone and like I'm giving you a lil hug and a lil squeeze whenever you need it. I think you're going to like some of the things I have to say . . . 🤞

*Love, Olivia xoxo*

## My body happy manifesto

*By the time you've finished this book, I want you to:*

✦ **Start to feel good about your body and learn to love the skin you're in**

✦ **Prioritise health and remember that healthy looks different on everybody**

✦ **Appreciate your cute lil squishy, cuddly bits**

✦ **Embrace your 'essence'**

✦ **Understand that you won't always adore what you see in the mirror and that's totally normal**

✦ **Be your own best friend and be kinder to yourself when you're having a down day**

✦ **Understand different food groups and the importance of nutrition and a balanced diet (treats included!)**

✦ **Know when to tune out negative comments from other people about your body**

✦ **Learn that comparing yourself to other people is only going to hurt you**

✦ **Make your own physical and mental health self-care a priority**

## What's in my book

*There's so much in my book and I can't wait for you to read it all :)*

In the chapters that follow, I'll share a bit about my own story of **self-confidence** as well as, erm, a few embarrassing stories. ;)

We'll also talk about where to start when it comes to finding something you like about yourself, using my special self-confidence techniques: Cute Lil Formula and Three Lil Things. And, just so you know, it's not about shouting **'I LOVE MYSELF!'** from the rooftops (because I don't really wanna do that either 😆) – I'm going to show you how it's more about actually liking who you really are (your 'essence') and that this is much deeper than just your body and how you look.

We're going to talk about how your body type is not new and the things you dislike about yourself right now were actually trends at one point in time . . . It's even weirder than it sounds!

To round it all off, I'll share my 10 Life Lessons – the things that have taken me **YEARS** to realise and which I wish I'd known along the way. They've really helped me feel more confident in myself and around other people.

*Let's get started . . .*

# Section 1:
# Changing Bodies

## Your changing body

*Understanding puberty*

Our bodies are amazing and they're constantly changing, throughout our whole lives, for various reasons, including ageing, weight fluctuations, puberty, (if you want to become a mum one day) pregnancy and menopause (when your periods eventually stop).

**Puberty is the phase when your body changes and grows into an adult's body. For girls, it generally starts a bit earlier than boys. According to the NHS, the average age for puberty to start for girls is eleven. However, it's normal for puberty to begin at any point between the ages of eight and thirteen in girls. General health, nutrition and environmental factors can have an impact on the stages of puberty.**

While some of these changes are slow and subtle, some are most definitely not. The time of change during puberty can be really exciting. But it's also OK and totally normal if you're struggling with your body changing.

I know that any changes can be tricky to deal with, especially if you feel like you have no control over what's going on. Maybe you feel like you no longer recognise the person looking back at you from the mirror or you're self-conscious about the way your body's changing. Perhaps you've noticed how your friends' bodies are changing and keep wondering if you're 'normal'. If any of this sounds familiar, I hear you. And I know that it sucks to feel like that – believe me, I get it!

But I promise you now, you're not the first to feel like that, and you won't be the last either. Sometimes, understanding a lil bit about what's going on in your body can help. At least, when I was going through it all, understanding the process helped me to know why certain lumps and bumps developed.

♡ *Olivia says:*

**Our bodies aren't meant to be a perfect, smooth canvas. They also have amazing functions – and I don't just mean walking and running and allowing you to move, but oh so much more! 🫸🩹**

Now, you've probably learned a few things during sex education classes at school, but I honestly think sex ed just scratches the surface – the basics. Puberty is the first big change to happen, and sometimes it can take years to accept the bodily changes . . . **Keep reading to find out more.**

## Hormones

*The reason for every change happening in your body right now*

Wait, stop . . . I know this is spoken about all the time and I know you probably think it's boring. But hormones are the main cause of the changes to our bodies that we experience in life.

Think of hormones as chemical messengers carrying instructions from one set of cells in your body to another. They trigger puberty to start with, making your boobs grow and causing all the other changes to your body, and they can make you feel all sorts of different ways.

Another thing to know is that hormones and fat have an important link. We need fat on our bodies – without it, you can't have a period or experience the fun lil changes puberty brings.

Puberty itself is triggered by the hormone HQ of your **brain,** the hypothalamus, releasing certain hormones. When your ovaries produce the **sex hormone oestrogen,** it kicks off one of the first signs of puberty in some girls – the development of your boobs . . .

## Boobs

*Boobs, boobies, nungas, melons, bee stings . . . (I'm not sure the editors will appreciate me mentioning any more, so moving swiftly on!)*

Breasts mainly consist of a combination of fat and glandular tissue, but they're **SO** much more than this. In the future, if you have a baby when you're older, you may choose to breastfeed, and the size of your boobs doesn't affect how much milk you make. All boobs have the same function, no matter how they look.

Growing a pair of boobs can be exciting, but it's also kind of weird when you think about it. They're essentially squishy lumps and kind of feel just like your belly or your thigh. They come in different shapes and sizes and have different nipple colours, sizes and placement. Try not to worry if yours are petite or bigger or a different shape or not matching – the combinations are endless – and, just like your fingerprint, no other pair of boobs will ever look just like yours.

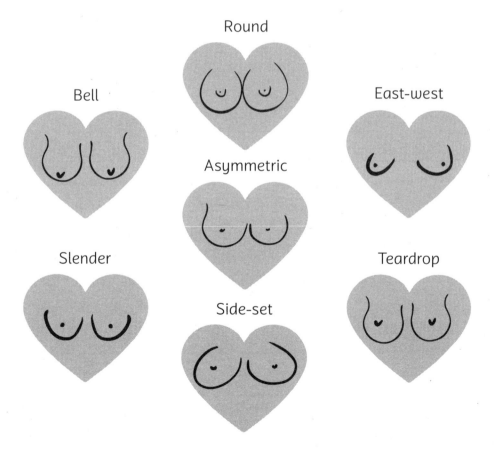

Round

Bell

East-west

Asymmetric

Slender

Teardrop

Side-set

Boobs can still grow up to the age of twenty-one, and even after that they change when you're older due to pregnancy, breastfeeding, weight fluctuations and, in later years, menopause.

♡ *Olivia says:*

**I always had small girlies until I was nineteen, and then by the time I was twenty-one, they had literally tripled in size.**

I was a late-ish developer with my boobs and was always like, 'Please come in, boobs.' Bras, for me, are an obsession. I **LOVE** cute underwear sets soooooooo much and I always have, even when I was size AAA. It doesn't matter what you, your body or your boobs look like, I genuinely believe that pretty underwear can be a confidence game changer. I don't wear a cute set every day, and I definitely don't wear a cute set for anyone other than me. You don't even need a matching set to feel this way – sometimes just a bra that you like does the job. :) I still remember my first cute bra being a hand-me-down from a friend whose boobs were growing at double the rate of mine – **I loved it and it was perfect!**

*Olivia says:*

**If I ever feel rubbish, I put a cute set on, listen to music and dance (by myself, may I add 😄), and my confidence is improved. Or even pose in the mirror — but u can't stand there and pick urself apart when doing this — you have to pay attention to the things you do like and pose and do whatever makes YOU feel good.**

♥

## Body hair

*Pubes ... you've probably already realised that body hair is a major part of being a woman*

Why do we have pubes? Pubic hair actually serves a really important purpose, mainly to protect your delicate bits from bacteria, as well as keeping them at the right temperature. Clever, right?!

While some girls are happy for their body hair to grow free, others prefer to shave or wax. It goes without saying that whatever you do with your body hair is your own personal preference. NOBODY else, and I mean nobody, gets to have an opinion on it other than you, OK?

Body fluff is normal, promise. You may also find random hairs in places where you really weren't expecting it, such as on your thighs, around your belly button, on your nipples and between your boobs. All normal. If you don't want to leave these cheeky rogue hairs, you can carefully pluck them. However, never and I repeat, NEVER shave your nipples or boobs . . . During my teens, I took a razor and shaved everywhere, across my arms and even on my chest. Worst idea ever!! The hair grew back, all prickly and stubbly, which was really uncomfortable for a while. I never made that mistake again.

**Ingrown hairs:** Raised, sometimes itchy bumps where the hair has grown back into the skin, usually caused by shaving.

I also used to over shave – like, every single day! I caused myself terrible razor burn and ingrown hairs, which are a common part of shaving – but annoying. When my skin was itchy and painful from over shaving, I used to pick at it too, which didn't help. Believe me, I know how hard it can be to get used to dealing with body hair. But I've made all the mistakes so hopefully you don't have to!

I have finally mastered the art of shaving – if I do say so myself. ☺ So here are my tips for having baby-soft skin:

✦ **Before you shave, exfoliate with an exfoliating mitt or gloves**

✦ **In your sensitive areas, make sure you shave in the direction of the hair growth, never upwards**

✦ **Keep your razor dry and clean to avoid any bad bacteria**

✦ **Moisturise afterwards with something gentle**

✦ **Try your hardest not to shave every day! I promise no one can see the lil stubbly bits**

# Periods

*Getting your first period is the moment when you might feel that you're finally a woman*

Whether you started years ago, have only just got your period or are still waiting for it to arrive, let's go through the basics. Some of these changes might affect how you feel about your body for a long time after. In one way, it can feel quite exciting to get your first period. But then there are lots of not-so-nice bits to it too, such as **stomach cramps** and feeling anxious about dealing with your flow. If you have heavy periods, you might be worrying about leaks. Let's go through the basics so that you understand everything that's going on.

You've probably noticed clear or white vaginal discharge in your knickers, which is something your body creates due to increases in the hormone oestrogen. Most girls get this discharge well before they get their first period.

Try not to worry if some of your friends have started their periods already and you feel left behind; it will happen in good time. Getting your first period can also be scary, even if you've been expecting it.

28

My own periods were insanely irregular through my teen years and still are now, sometimes. Whether it's your first period or you've already been having them for years, the stress of getting your period unexpectedly is universal, especially when you're at school or away from home. The main thing is to be prepared. Having a lil period stash of essentials is always a good idea.

Medically speaking, your period is the regular shedding of blood from your uterus through your vagina. You may have bright red blood or just spotting with red-brown discharge – both are normal and nothing to worry about. Depending on your cycle, your period will come every 21 to 35 days and can last between 2 to 7 days, but periods can be irregular.

My first period, when I was fourteen, was **stresssssssful.** I was staying at a friend's house, far away from home. I only had tampons, as that was all she gave me, and I couldn't get to a shop . . . Nightmare. I didn't know what I was doing, and that whole day, I walked around with a loose tampon in my knickers. Thankfully, I've mastered the art of tampon insertion now . . . **Woo!!**

If you do want to use tampons during your period, you might need a bit of practice. I remember talking to my friends about it and they all used different methods. One of my friends put one of her legs on the toilet seat, one put a mirror on the floor so that she could see what she was doing and one would squat while giving herself a pep talk.

**30**

## MY STEP-BY-STEP GUIDE TO USING TAMPONS

If you're struggling with tampons, here are my lil top tips (if you're already a whizz at this, then feel free to skip):

- Using tampons with applicators is easier when you're just starting out.
- Choose the right absorbency. If you've only just started your periods, a thinner tampon with lighter absorbency may be more comfortable.
- If you're nervous, or getting used to using tampons, you may want to use a thin pantyliner or pad with a tampon in case of leaks.
- Find a comfortable position – try sitting on the toilet with your knees apart.
- Slowly insert the top half of the applicator into your vagina, aiming towards the small of your back, not straight up. Push it up GENTLY until your fingers are touching your skin.
- Pull the applicator out and throw it away – never flush or you may end up with a blocked toilet!
- Check the tampon is comfortable – you shouldn't be able to feel it when walking or sitting.
- If you need to readjust it, pop a finger in and GENTLY move it around until you feel comfortable.
- Ideally, you should change your tampon every four to six hours and never leave one in longer than eight hours.
- Try not to worry about removing a tampon – it may feel a bit uncomfortable, but by staying relaxed and not tensing your vagina, you'll find it much easier! Remember: NO TENSING!
- Dispose of used tampons in a bin.

Before your period, you may notice you are feeling extra down or annoyed about lil things. This is PMS (premenstrual syndrome), which is caused by extra hormones flowing through your body. Some people feel it more intensely than others.

Your period may be super painful to start with, and you may suffer some of the following:

✦ **Stomach cramps**

✦ **Feeling lightheaded or faint**

✦ **Headaches**

✦ **Nausea or sickness**

✦ **A funny tummy, aka period poops** 💩

I understand how awful it is to suffer period pain . . . I used to have such terrible cramps and would feel sick, and once I even fainted. It was so hard. When you feel that bad (urrggh), the best thing to do is just crawl under the duvet with:

✦ **A hot-water bottle**

✦ **A bar of chocolate**

✦ **Reality TV**

*Olivia says:*

**When you have period pain and feel yuk, see it as an excuse to have a massive pamper sesh.**

If you're really struggling with period pain and other symptoms around your period, the NHS recommends asking to see your GP, who can offer support and possible treatments to help you.

**FROM MAYVRILL, OUR COUNSELLOR:**
Puberty is an example of 'mind and body' as it's not just the body that changes but also the brain, which begins to mature during this time.

## Spots

*I know how upsetting it is when you look in the mirror and see those lil red dots and bumps appear*

If I'm completely honest, I found my skin changing to be a lil heartbreaking experience . . . I don't feel like that now, but I did back then. I was thirteen when — **\*ta-dah\*** — it felt like an invasion on my face: the lil bumpies all over my forehead and the red puffy ones on my cheeks . . . Argh! And I was obsessed with researching a cure, which meant endless hours of sleep lost and plans cancelled because I didn't want anyone to see my face. I didn't even want my family to see. :(

Between you and me, I think I felt embarrassed. But, looking back now, I wanna give younger me a big ol' hug because there's no need to be embarrassed! Just like we can't control our heart beating, we can't control how our skin is going to be, and no matter how much you clean your skin and wash your face, your skin is gonna do what it wants.

> The NHS says that about 95% of people aged eleven to thirty are affected by acne in some way and that it's most common in girls between the ages of fourteen to seventeen. If this is you, you're absolutely NOT the only one.

You probably already know that acne is linked to changes in your hormone levels. Also, around your time of the month, you might suffer breakouts – just another 'blessing' of being a woman. ;)

## Time to get scientific . . .

> All the extra hormones during puberty cause the grease-producing glands next to hair follicles in your skin to produce larger amounts of oil (abnormal sebum), which can make a skin bacterium called P. acnes trigger inflammation and pus. Hormones also thicken the inner lining of the hair follicle, causing pores to become blocked.

Just so you know, cleaning the skin doesn't help to remove this blockage. Also, the NHS says there's no evidence that poor diet or poor hygiene cause acne.

If someone is ever nasty about your skin, it will always say more about them and their character than about you. Being mean for no reason is an ick.

### Olivia says:

**If anyone tries to 'blame' you for having spots, telling you that you're eating the wrong food or not washing enough, don't listen . . . just show them this page!**

At the end of the day, if you're stuck overthinking what other people think about you, remember this . . . It's not about if they like you, it's about if YOU like them!

> ## Olivia says:
>
> **So u have the cutie lil red bumps on ur face and so what? It DOESN'T TAKE AWAY FROM UR BEAUTY even though I know it can feel that way and like no one gets it and no one understands – but I do, and maybe my words can make u feel less alone? And knowing it will get better might give u a lil more hope? ♡₊˚**

When I was around fifteen, I went to a **dermatologist** and I remember, so clearly, sitting there as she removed the make-up that had taken me two hours to carefully apply. The room went silent, my mum gasped and I tried to hold back the tears as the dermatologist agreed that yes, I had 'bad skin'. :( I tried different medications over the years but still struggled.

These days, I don't get spots like I used to but I still get the odd one. Spots aren't necessarily age specific; they come when and where they want – on your face, across your shoulders and on your back. I even used to get spots on my boobs . . . Mmm, what a time!

When I had 'bad skin', I also made it so much worse by picking at my skin obsessively. Yep, I'm a picker! In fact, I was diagnosed with something called skin picking disorder.

**What is skin picking disorder?**
Most people occasionally pick at their skin. But you may have skin picking disorder (aka excoriation disorder) if you can't stop picking at your skin, particularly at spots or scars. You may even cause your skin to bleed or bruise by picking it. Help yourself by keeping your hands busy (try a stress squeezer ball) or having a friend or family member around when washing your face, and if you're worried, speak to a doctor.

**There's no magic cure for spots. I know it can suck to hear that. And yes, skincare can help – but only so much. And that's OK, I promise.**

Here are some of my top **skincare tips:**

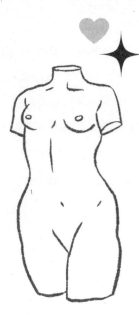

✦ **No sleeping in make-up**

✦ **Avoid harsh chemicals as they can hurt your skin barrier (the outermost layer of your skin)**

✦ **Don't be afraid of moisturising**

- ✦ **Please, please don't make my mistake of damaging your skin, using crazy amounts of tea tree oil or really harsh chemicals**

- ✦ **In fact, don't overuse any products as they can leave your skin dry and flaky . . . WISH I'd known that** 🤓

And here are some essentials you should have in your **spot care package:**

✦ **An oil-free moisturiser – literally your skincare BFF** 🫶

✦ **A gentle face wash – your saviour, morning and night**

✦ **Azelaic acid – a tiny pea-sized amount of this can help with the lil bumpies**

✦ **An antiseptic healing cream like Sudocrem – my OG for red spots (and if you've picked your skin, carefully apply it to help with healing)**

✦ **A good concealer, the same shade as your skin, to use instead of foundation – so you can dot every lil spot with it and it won't feel too cakey**

## Greasy hair

*Just as your skin feels more oily, your hair can feel greasier too*

First of all, greasier hair isn't as bad as you think, because the oils on your scalp are actually good for your hair – *yay* – but it does mean that hair washing days will become more frequent. At one point, I needed to wash my hair every day and, I'm not gonna lie, that wasn't fun. That was before my discovery of dry shampoo – my ultimate fave haircare thing **EVER.** But don't worry, because once you're through your teen years, your hair won't be so greasy . . . I can go three to six days between washing it these days . . . **Woo!**

Here are my top lil tips for greasy hair:

✦ **Try not to wash it every day as it's not great for your hair – although obviously you know your hair best and, if this works for you, carry on.**

- ✦ I used a detox shampoo during my extra greasy hair stage.

- ✦ Only use conditioner on the ends of your hair, not your roots.

- ✦ Use dry shampoo. I can still remember when my friends and I discovered dry shampoo – it will give you a day or two extra between washes and also gives you loads of volume – I LOVE IT.

- ✦ I now use Nizoral Anti-Dandruff Shampoo, because I also have psoriasis (a skin condition that Kim Kardashian also has, if that makes it sound more exciting!) and I think it really helps with grease too.

- ✦ Find cute lil hairstyles for a greasy hair day: a slicked-back bun; half up, half down . . . the list is endless and the world is your oyster. 📖

**Weird fact:** my hair completely changed during puberty.
I went from straight to curly, which I found very exciting.
Also, my hair got darker and, as a blondie, that meant I
wanted highlights. Oh boy, have I had a few hair disasters
– from being stripey to completely frazzled. 😅

Here are my lil general **hair care** tips:

✦ **Whatever you do, DON'T use too much heat and, if you can, use a heat protector – aged thirteen, I didn't know heat damage was a thing and I cringe thinking back to how I'd clamp the straightener on the ends of my hair for so long it sizzled away.**

✦ **A lil hair cream on wet hair or oil on dry hair can really help smooth things out and make your hair softer.**

✦ **If you have curls, find a curl mousse, cream or gel you like . . . everyone's curls are different so find a routine that works for you.**

# Growing taller

## Puberty is all about growwwwing . . .

After looking in, like, a hundred shops, you finally found
the most perfect pair of jeans . . . and now you realise
that you grew in the space of what feels like a week and
they don't fit. No, stop, this is heartbreaking!

Personally, I was a slowwwww grower. But if you're
growing faster than you can keep a check on, see it as an
excuse to go find another, even cuter pair of jeans.

Weird fact – during puberty, your hands and feet tend to
grow first, usually shortly before you have a growth spurt.
Bodies are weird!

**Growth spurt:** A normal part of growing up,
when you grow very quickly. Growth spurts
happen at different ages but especially during
puberty. Most girls have a growth spurt
between the ages of ten and fourteen, so
if you're suddenly getting taller, you know
why. Honestly, everyone's so different, it can
happen whenever your body feels like it, and
you may notice some growing pains too.

You can actually grow 8 cm in a year . . . **amazing!** But you might feel awkward if your arms and legs suddenly seem waaay longer than they used to be. Hello to walking into corners, doors and banging your hips on tables . . . Owww.

With all that growing to do, it makes sense that teenagers your age need **A LOT** of sleep – you're not lazy, you're just growing. Everyone grows at different rates, and if your friends are all shooting up and leaving you behind, be patient; you'll get taller too . . . in your own time. I'm a short gal (love that for me!) and I come from a short family, so any growth spurts were exciting. Actually, I was still growing when I was nineteen, after an eating disorder at eighteen temporarily stunted my growth. It was my dad who first noticed that I'd grown and he was very excited – **soo cute!**

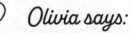

## Olivia says:

**Embrace your height – or lack of it – and how it makes you special. If you're tall – well, model vibes . . . hellooooo! If you're a short girly, like me, think of it as cute.**

# Wider hips

## *It can feel weird to have new curves*

As your pelvis (the large bone across your hips) grows, you might notice your hips gradually getting wider. You probably already know that the widening of your pelvis and hips is to prepare you for having babies when you're an adult, if that's what you choose to do.

Some girls love their new curves, and if that's you, I'm so happy and excited for you! Believe me, it can also feel weird to have curves where there used to be none, and if it takes you a lil time to adjust to the changes – that's OK. We **all** are different and genetics play a major role in our overall shape: some of us have smaller hips or big boobs or broad shoulders . . . The list goes on and the combinations are endless . . . Just like there are loadsss of different types of flowers, there are soooo many different body shapes.

### *Olivia says:*

🥀✨ Your body type has been a trend — you just weren't around to see it. ✨🥀

Your body type may not be trending in your lifetime but it 100% already has been before. Your body type isn't something new.

Your ancestors have passed down their characteristics to ✨you✨.

You share the same features as your ancestors and many women and men before you. There's nothing wrong with you — if anything, these features were passed on because of love, so do with that info what you will. 😎🫶

## Weight gain

*During the time when your hips and boobs are growing, you may also gain weight*

I cannot say this enough: weight gain is a natural and normal part of puberty. Your body will instruct fat cells (did you know that fat is actually called adipose tissue?) to go to certain areas, like your thighs and bum and even your lower tummy, to create essential fat stores – which will be used if you become pregnant in future years.

Women have a higher body fat percentage than men, and fat is very important for our hormones. That's why if you don't eat enough, your period can be disrupted and might even stop.

When I was younger, I was always so scared about gaining weight. I thought that once I started to become a woman, I had to restrict everything that I ate. As I've already mentioned, due to my disordered eating, I developed an **eating disorder.**

**FROM CHRISTINA, OUR DIETITIAN:**
**Disordered eating:** Irregular eating patterns that fall between healthy eating and a fully diagnosed eating disorder. Disordered eating behaviours may include avoiding certain foods, bingeing and exercising excessively. Getting support quickly is key to recovery.

**Eating disorders:** According to the NHS, an eating disorder is a mental health condition where you use the control of food to cope with feelings and other situations.

- Anyone can get an eating disorder, but teenagers between thirteen and seventeen are mostly affected
- With treatment, most people can recover from an eating disorder

**The most common eating disorders are:**
- Anorexia nervosa – trying to control your weight by not eating enough food, exercising too much or doing both
- Bulimia – losing control over how much you eat and then taking drastic action to not put on weight by vomiting
- Binge eating disorder – regularly eating large portions of food until you feel uncomfortably full, without feeling like you have any control
- Avoidant/restrictive food intake disorder – an eating or feeding disturbance such as a lack of interest in food or restricting certain types of food, leading to significant nutritional deficiency

Once I was in recovery and gaining weight again, I gained the fat back and the extra weight I always needed too, and sometimes I was sad about my squishy belly. But then I'd remind myself that it's just natural body fat and think about all the functions it serves – like regulating your hormones and hunger hormones, insulation, protecting your organs and your uterus. Think of it as a **squishy pillow** – just like your boobs – and having a lil extra squish makes you cuddly and soft. Or perhaps you're worrying about not having the curves you want? Throughout this book you'll learn what makes you you, and how to feel good and healthy in the body you have.

♡ *Olivia says:*

**Being squishy means being cuddly and that, to me, sounds amazing. I love how soft my skin is and how cuddly my body is, and seriously anyone who has the pleasure to have a big ol' cuddle with me: quite frankly, ur welcome. ☺**

I was worried about what boys would think too . . . stupid, I know. 😄 Actually, since gaining weight, I haven't noticed a difference when it comes to boys – only in myself, in that I'm more confident now. I came to the conclusion that boys would need to like my cute lil belly because it's part of me. And if they didn't, then that was their loss (haha) . . . No, but seriously. Plus, if every single human ate the same and did the same exercise, we'd still all look different from each other!!

♡ **Olivia says:**

**If someone could wave a magic wand 🪄 and get rid of my lil belly, I genuinely would say, 'Absolutely NOTTT!!' I finally feel like I belong in my body and that it fits me. 🤗 I'm curvy now and not in a 'perfect' way, but that's perfectly OK with ME. 🤗🩵**

## Stretch marks

*Now let's talk about some of the body changes that nobody ever seems to mention, even though they happen to almost every girl...*

First up . . . stretch marks, which are a really **normal** part of puberty for most girls – and some boys too – but which can come as, erm, a bit of a shock. While skin is pretty stretchy, it can reach its limits when you're growing super-fast. So stretchies appear around your hips, bottom, thighs or stomach as a series of wriggly streaks. Depending on your skin colour, they can be pink, red, purple, reddish-brown or dark brown – and they may start off slightly raised and itchy.

**I FULLY get it if you feel self-conscious, because my lil stretchies were my first ever BIG insecurity growing up. When I spotted my first stretchie, I was around eleven. I never knew they were just part of becoming a woman. I'm not gonna lie, I honestly thought only older and pregnant people got them . . . Was this just me?!**

I guess that I just never saw young women on social media or in magazines or on TV with stretchies. None of my friends had them then either, so I felt like my body was betraying me and I was the only one! Obviously, I was wrong . . . Slowly, my friends got them, but I still felt I was the only one with so many on their bum, and I truly felt this way for yearsss. I slowly came to the conclusion that it's just part of having curves. I have a bottom, I have thighs and no, they are not completely airbrushed and smooth to look at – but they are squishy and soft and **strong.** And this is the reality of home-grown curves – it happens, it's real, I'm human.

Honestly, I still don't think I **LOVE** my stretchies (yet!), but I can genuinely say that I've accepted them, I don't care that they're there and I don't spend ANY time worrying about them. They're just there because my thighs and bottom grew, and stretchies are a part of growing curves. In a way, they tell the story of the changes in my body. If me accepting them can bring anyone comfort, then that makes all the struggles of accepting them worth it. ⚡

If you're struggling with your **stretchies**, here are my lil tips:

♥ **I used every behind-the-counter product I could find on my stretchies, and to be completely honest, I'm not sure how much any of them helped – but it's still worth a go if it makes you feel better. Also, they smell good and make your skin feel soft, so still a win!**

♥ **Remember that stretchies are genetic – there's nothing wrong with you if you get them, and they will eventually die down a bit and get less red and raised.**

## Olivia says:

**I don't want to see filtered and smoothed and altered.**

**I want to see real, reality, living people.**

**I don't want to wish to look airbrushed.**

**I want to wish to be on the beach with the warm wind in my hair.**

**I want to dream of love and a family and my goals, and not my body shrinking and smoothing and 'improving'.**

# Cellulite

## Cellulite is a normal part of becoming a woman for nearly all girls

Cellulite is one of those other lil changes that can happen in puberty which nobody ever really prepares you for. It can be a shock to see a change in the texture of your skin and, for me, that was definitely the case.

Not actually sure what cellulite is? It's the lil dimples on the backs of your thighs or bottom and it can appear anywhere there is fat. Pinch the skin around your upper thigh. If it looks lumpy, that's cellulite. But it's really nothing to worry about – it's a normal part of growing up for girls, and some boys have it too.

However, only around 10% of men have cellulite! This is because men and women have a different structure between their fat cells and connective tissue. In women, they are structured vertically, in a circular structure in rows going up and down, so if their fat cells are against the layer of skin, they give the dimpled appearance of cellulite. In men, this tissue has a criss-cross structure, which holds their fat cells more in place, which is why they are less likely to have cellulite.

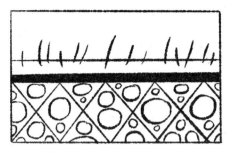

Male cells

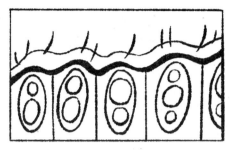

Female cells

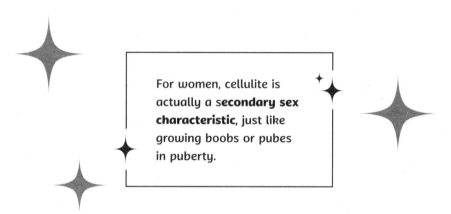

For women, cellulite is actually a **secondary sex characteristic**, just like growing boobs or pubes in puberty.

**Just so you know, you can have cellulite if you're slim or if you're curvier. I've been both and still had it when I was suffering from an eating disorder and was dangerously underweight.**

You might read about 'magic' cures for cellulite, from creams and oils to special massage techniques. Honestly, though, there's nothing that can stop you from getting cellulite and there's nothing wrong with it either. In fact, up to 90% of women have it somewhere on their bodies.

**So, repeat after me . . .**
**It.**
**Is.**
**Totally.**
**Normal.**

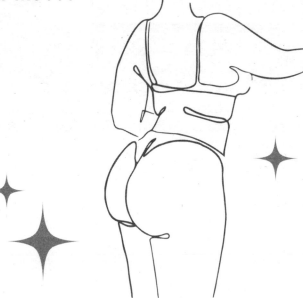

♡ *Olivia says:*

I have cellulite and lil lumps and bumps and curves. I'm not as smooth as glass. I'm as soft and snuggly as a cloud, and I just think that sounds so cute tbh.

## My story

*As soon as I started being aware that my body was changing and I was becoming a woman, I thought that I had a life of dieting destined for me . . .*

Growing up, I was surrounded by diet culture — not just from TV, magazines and social media, but also mainly at home. At home is where it all started for me.

***Diet culture is a set of cultural myths about health, weight and food.***

My first experience with becoming conscious of my weight was when I was only ten and still at primary school. I developed anxiety and, as this was before mental health was spoken about so openly, I had no idea what was going on when I felt so nervous that my stomach would hurt. I know now these were panic attacks, which, for me, meant that I couldn't eat — and if I was extremely anxious, I would projectile vomit. I was so ashamed, I felt miserable and I knew it was my mind causing all this, but no else knew how I was feeling.

**FROM MAYVRILL, OUR COUNSELLOR:**
A qualified therapist can provide tools to encourage a helpful way of thinking throughout the transition of puberty. Many local authorities have free counselling provision for young people, usually from ages eleven to twenty-five.

I was aware of my lil round belly and had no thoughts about it. But now that my anxiety was making it hard for me to eat, I was soon looking in the mirror and realising that it was gone. By the time summer came around that year, mentally I was doing better and I started eating three meals again, and the weight was coming back. One summer afternoon I was in my favourite frilly denim bikini and roller skates when my grandmother and my mum were having a conversation about my body. They were talking about the weight I'd lost, and even though I hadn't put much thought into how my body had changed, now all of a sudden I was much more aware of it. Soon, my lil round belly was back. I didn't realise my body would continue to gain weight. And this time, I had different feelings about it. I felt betrayed by my body. I had wanted it to stay how it was. This was my first experience of losing weight and gaining it back – a pattern I would soon become very much accustomed to.

Sadly, **diet culture** had a strong grip on my mother, like so many other women. I looked up to her, growing up, and came to the conclusion that, at some point, I would have to start eating like her for the rest of my life. The summer before secondary school was just that. I mistakenly thought that dieting was part of becoming a woman (spoiler – I couldn't have been more wrong 🐼).

Going to secondary school meant I could get away from home, which was something I so desperately craved. I had my heart set on going to an all-girls boarding school, and once I started there, I realised that when I was at school, I would start to feel better. At school, I would eat when I was hungry and I would especially eat sweets and chocolate – something I was not usually allowed much of at home, growing up. Easter chocolate was taken away, and on holidays I was reminded not to eat too much, told I was greedy, told to slow down or told I didn't need to finish whatever I was eating even if I was in fact . . . just **hungry.** Weight was a big topic at home. It was also around this age that I first noticed lil dimples (cellulite) and stretchies appearing on my bottom, as I started to grow curves. Not realising that this was a normal part of puberty and becoming a woman, I was horrendously embarrassed. It even got to the point that during a family holiday, when I was twelve, I asked my younger sister Eloise, then eight, to film me walking in three different ways so that I could work out which walk was better for hiding my cellulite. It breaks my heart to remember this – for both myself and my younger sister, who just wanted to go to the beach! But I did not. I wouldn't go into the sea in case anyone saw me; I felt so insecure and humiliated just by living in my own body. To think how much joy I missed out on . . .

All through my teen years, I was dieting. I fell into a loop of eating lots at school and then dieting at home on the weekends. I didn't know this back then, but this is called yo-yo dieting and **it can make your body not function properly** – as do all forms of extreme dieting.

**Metabolism:** Chemical changes in your body, some of which break down food, creating energy for your body to use.

**FROM CHRISTINA, OUR DIETITIAN:**
A balanced diet is essential for maintaining good health and wellbeing, and each food group provides a variety of essential nutrients that contribute to overall health. Your body needs a variety of foods and amounts to function properly, and a well-balanced diet typically includes a combination of macronutrients (carbohydrates, proteins and fats) and micronutrients (vitamins and minerals).

Every day is **different** and that's OK!
It's healthy to go out for a meal and enjoy
a pizza, as well as having a balanced
plate of food like this one.

**Fruit and vegetables:**
You can get a wide range of vitamins
and minerals into your diet by
eating lots of fruits and vegetables.
Different colours in fruits and
vegetables often mean they have
different nutrient profiles. Dairy
products or dairy alternatives,
fortified foods and supplements
can also help you get more
calcium, which is essential for
our bone health, and vitamin D.
Fruit and vegetables can make
up to half of a balanced plate.

**Fibre:**
Fibre is crucial for digestive health
and can be found in wholegrains,
fruits, vegetables, legumes and nuts.

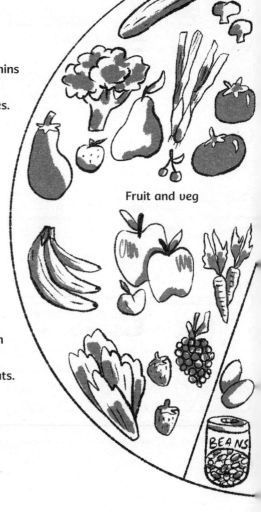

Fruit and veg

### Carbohydrates:

Carbohydrates are the body's main source of energy. They are found in foods like grains, fruits and vegetables.

Carbohydrates

### Hydration:

Water is essential for lots of bodily functions, including digestion, nutrient absorption and temperature regulation.

Fats

### Fats:

Fats are important for energy storage and hormone production, and they are crucial for brain functioning.

### Proteins:

Proteins are essential for building and repairing tissue, including muscles, as well as supporting your immune system. Sources of protein include meat, poultry, fish, eggs, dairy products, legumes, nuts and seeds. Proteins can be up to one third of a balanced plate.

Proteins

As time went on, the dieting lasted longer and became more extreme. I became even more conscious of my weight. I also had undiagnosed ADHD, which meant that I was very impulsive and did things without thinking, which always landed me in a LOT (a LOT!!) of trouble at school. I got put on every report, and at one point I got suspended. Soon, school was no longer my safe place, and at home I felt alone and terribly, terribly sad.

**ADHD (attention deficit hyperactivity disorder): A neurodiversity disorder which affects your ability to pay attention and control your impulses. People with ADHD may:**
- Be forgetful
- Be disorganised
- Talk a lot
- Interrupt
- Fidget and find it hard to stay still

**FROM MAYVRILL, OUR COUNSELLOR:**
Neuroscientists continue to study how our brains can affect our behaviour and mental health. Therapy can help people with a diagnosis of ADHD or ADD to understand the science and also themselves. Effective techniques such as mindfulness can help to create calm, and other tools include appropriate nutrition, getting adequate sleep and accessing local support networks.

Although on the surface I was loud and bubbly, I was such an unhappy lil bean deep down. I hated the way I looked and would stare at myself in the mirror for, like, three hours to figure out what was 'wrong' with me.

At the start of sixth form, I finally got diagnosed with ADHD. But, after being put on medication, things took a turn for the worse because the medication affected my appetite and I lost more weight than ever. I had never seen myself so thin. Struggling with my studies, I left school and moved home, where I started at a sixth form college nearby.

I needed a new start, but although I stopped taking the ADHD medication, it had ruined my relationship with my body, and my relationship with food was at an all-time low. I was having counselling, and a new therapist I was seeing started to listen to me about my insecurities. It wasn't just one thing about myself that I disliked – it was **EVERYTHING.** My eyes, my hairline, my spots, my thighs, my belly, every small lil thing . . . I was so self-critical and I'd spend hours trying to 'fix' what I perceived to be my flaws by applying layers and layers of make-up and only wearing specific clothes if they hid parts I didn't like.

**The sad truth is that I hated myself. What I didn't know then was that I was suffering from body dysmorphic disorder.**

**Body dysmorphic disorder (BDD):** A mental health condition that causes the sufferer to spend a lot of time worrying about flaws in their appearance, which are often unnoticeable to others. It can affect people of any age but is most common in teens and young adults. Symptoms can include:

- Looking at your reflection in the mirror A LOT and examining your appearance – in a negative way
- Constantly comparing your appearance to other people
- Avoiding social events and photos
- Seeking cosmetic surgery
- Always asking other people for reassurance about how you look
- Excessive grooming
- Restricted eating
- Anxiety
- Depression
- Intrusive thoughts
- Compulsive behaviour

**FROM MAYVRILL, OUR COUNSELLOR:**
BDD can be evoked and perpetuated by negative thoughts, which can culminate into a serious mental health disorder. There are several ways to support and improve this disorder, and the mental health organisation Mind has several strategies available for free on their website. Therapy techniques such as CBT can also be effective in promoting a healthier self-belief.

**I remember hearing the symptoms for the first time, in therapy, and it was this moment where I realised . . . 'OMG, this isn't normal?! This is a condition?! So I can get better?!' It was a lil glimmer of hope.**

And then there was food. I felt so much shame around food and was secretly struggling with disordered eating. I felt so ashamed about the way I was behaving, and out of control – I didn't know how to behave or what to do to feel better. At this point, I was at college and had made new friends who also struggled with their relationship with food, and we bonded over this, but not in a positive way. One day, on YouTube, I came across an influencer talking about how she'd supposedly 'fixed' her relationship with food. I felt so out of control and was starving myself so I was constantly hungry, but at the time I couldn't understand how destructive this was. The influencer spoke about an app she used to track her calories and how many she ate in a day. With the knowledge I now have, I can see that she in fact had not fixed her relationship with food, but instead had swapped one eating disorder out for another.

But I didn't understand that at the time. So I sat on the floor outside my bathroom, went into the App Store on my phone and found the exact app she was using. Upon downloading it, I had a gut feeling that this was a **bad idea** – I hesitated as I put in my details. But I also thought it would help me control my eating, which I was desperate to do, so I chose the thought of losing weight over my instinct (I literally was going about it in the worst way possible – I had no idea!).

The thing is that two people could start the same diet, and while one of them might be fine, the other might fall into an eating disorder. And I was the second type of person. That's why following online diet advice is **SO** dangerous – and honestly, it's what tipped me over the edge. You don't know someone else's relationship with food, and eating disorders really make you very delulu, so while someone online may be very convincing, their advice could be harmful. Sadly, for me, it was extremely harmful.

**That summer, things were going from bad to worse** as I'd become very strict with the calorie app and logged every single calorie that passed my lips. My obsession with food grew. (Did you know that a big symptom of an eating disorder is that you're always thinking about food? I always assumed that it was the other way around – I found out the hard way.)

I managed to hide from my family how little I was eating. I remember conversations with my mum about how she could go a whole day without eating. I know now this wasn't healthy behaviour, but at the time I found myself comparing what I ate to my mum, and made sure that every day I ate less than her. As summer went on, I became more and more a shell of myself. I'd lost lots of weight, my skin was dry and I grew lanugo. I stopped talking to friends and so many more things which all kept getting worse.

**Lanugo:** A type of soft, fine body hair which is one of the side effects of anorexia nervosa, bulimia nervosa and other eating disorders. When someone doesn't have enough body fat to keep them warm, their body responds by growing fine hair to help insulate them.

At the end of the summer, my eating issues were so painfully obvious to everyone and I was the most miserable I'd ever been. Everyone has future dreams that can motivate them, and for me this had been to have a family of my own – but now I wasn't even interested in that. I knew something had to **change,** but I wasn't ready.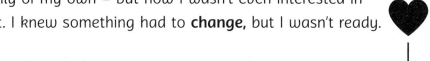

Behind the scenes, my parents had arranged for me to go into a special clinic and I was told I was going to see a new therapist, as my current one had mentioned that my issues were too much for them to deal with alone. I was counting the calories of ibuprofen and chewing gum. At this point it wasn't about weight – it became much more than that.

When I arrived in the clinic, I knew this was unlike anywhere I'd been previously. A clinic for mental health? A clinic for eating disorders? It dawned on me that it was the latter. The shiny metal lift door opened and, as a curvy lady with blonde hair calmly walked out and introduced herself to me, I burst into tears. I then understood that my mum was coming in to talk with her too . . .

I was diagnosed with bulimia and then, later, with anorexia too. At first, I wasn't open to any of their help. But as my symptoms got worse, it slowly dawned on me that actually I needed to change. I wanted to get some of my life back. At this point I didn't see any friends – I went to college for my classes and then straight home. My hair was falling out, I lost my period, I started having even stranger habits with food – about texture and temperature – and I had a blood test which revealed that I had reduced bone marrow function, which is something that happens if you don't eat enough . . . I'd had no idea!!!

The turning point when I finally decided I would accept some of their help was walking back home from college. I had no energy in me and the only thing keeping me going was repeating 'calories, calories, calories' after every step, because I knew that I was burning calories by moving. I knew this was insanely out of character and I just wanted a bit of me back, but I didn't know how to get there.

At first, during my treatment, I was very stubborn. Everyone at the clinic will forever have the most special, special place in my heart. My psychiatrist finally managed to convince me to try anti-anxiety medication, which really helped. She also arranged for me to have appointments with the dietitians. I will always scream from the rooftops about how much I love dietitians! They changed everything for me by teaching me about the science of food and healthy eating.

Due to my disordered eating and eating disorders, I'd cut out different food groups at different points over the years. The dietitians helped me understand, from a scientific point of view, the importance of each food group and why each one, including fat, was an essential part of a healthy, balanced diet. Learning this was groundbreaking for me.

My dietitians also told me their own **food stories.** They'd tell me about their Sunday mornings with their families – about how they'd eat a croissant, and maybe even a second croissant if they were still hungry. And how they would make a sandwich with butter and a filling. I got to hear all about their memories of having food with their families. They taught me how to make a balanced plate of food and how some food rules are healthy and some are not.

My mum was a huge pillar of support for me during this time, but I also struggled with her eating habits. I realised I had to set my own example of a good relationship with food. I've always wanted my own family in the future, and I would daydream about the memories we could make together, going to the beach on a hot summer day and having an ice cream together. I wanted to be strong enough to show them what my body was like without dieting and by living in balance.

**Both my parents were so very helpful, going out to get specific foods from specific brands that I deemed OK to eat. My mum would sit with me for hours and hours, talking with me.**

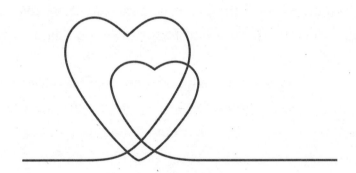

I'd always had long, thick hair, but because I hadn't been eating properly and hadn't been getting the nutrients I needed, it looked like a sheer curtain. You don't see how bad the damage is to your hair until you start healing – it will then start falling out, because your hair is the last to get nutrients, and if you haven't been eating enough, your hair is not as important to your body as keeping your organs functioning!

Some days in recovery were horrible, and some days felt like a beacon of light and hope that things would one day be OK again and that maybe, just maybe, I'd be able to eat like a 'normal' person. On the very bad days, I would hide under my duvet, not wanting the sunlight to touch my eyes or anything, not even water, to pass my lips, and I would refuse to talk. On these days, it was only my mum who could get through to me.

I don't actually have any pics of me from that time because I absolutely hated how I looked. Losing all that weight damaged my lil body and my brain (it actually shrinks in anorexia) and I still hated my reflection. About a year and a bit after recovering, I saw a snippet of a video of me just in PJ bottoms that my sister got on my phone without me realising. I was shocked. I didn't remember myself looking like that. Because the truth is that, at the time, I never felt like I ever got small enough. I remember my parents rubbing their fingers on my back while I was wearing a thick dressing gown, and feeling their fingers bump over my ribs from the back. I remember my legs were so weak that they would shake while I was walking down the stairs. But I still wore big, baggy clothes and covered myself up because I never thought that I was thin enough. Now I can see how utterly miserable I was and, above all, I'm **SO** glad I didn't go any lower . . . I'm so, so grateful I didn't cause any more harm.

My recovery from anorexia was very gradual, but from the middle of 2020, I started to turn a corner. Due to Covid, my A level exams were cancelled and I was at home with nothing to do but focus on getting better. During that time, I made **HUGE** progress. I wanted to be healthy and I'd learned, during my treatment, that healthy looked different on everybody and it didn't have to mean being unnaturally thin for my body shape.

Dreams of going on dates and seeing my friends without being preoccupied by food made me excited to recover. I wanted to live a life where there was space for **EVERYTHING** – space for salad, space for cupcakes, space for fish, space for ice cream, space for everything . . . My first meal in recovery when I didn't count the calories was on 13 June 2020, and it was something that I thought would not be possible for me. I thought I would only be able to maintain living in recovery if I counted calories for the rest of my life. I still honestly feel so proud of this, like my heart swells! After this, it was a cascading effect and I gradually stopped counting completely. I became so obsessed with numbers when I was ill – I've always loved maths, but this was too much. The numbers controlled me completely – my day, my mood, my food, my everything.

Thanks to eating properly again, I began to have **more energy.** I was even able to go for **walks** out of the house without feeling faint. Bit by bit, I was gradually getting my life back. I remember the feeling, one day during the summer of 2020, of breaking out into a run for the first time in what felt like ages, and not to be cringey, but I just felt **so many sensations.** The air running through my hair and my feet hitting the ground after each step. **It was just so beautiful.**

I guess, along the way, I had lost all joy and hope, and it was just these lil moments when I could see how amazing recovery was – and they were truly the best feelings ever. Recovery isn't linear – it's always got its bumps. But it will always be worth it.

**FROM CHRISTINA, OUR DIETITIAN:**
Weight redistribution after gaining weight will vary from person to person, and factors such as genetics, body composition, hormonal changes, sex, age and day-to-day routines can influence how and where the body stores fat. The body prioritises healing and recovery, so changes may not occur uniformly. As weight is restored, the body works to repair internal organs and systems first. With continued progress in recovery, you may observe more noticeable changes in fat distribution. Specific timelines and outcomes vary, but usually after a good six months of maintaining a healthy weight due to a consistent and balanced diet, you will begin to see changes to your body as it is able to use the energy more efficiently. Muscles start to strengthen, and the fat stores will distribute more evenly around the whole body.

And so, you see, I struggled like sooo many other girls with my body image and so much with feeling cripplingly alone because of it. But somehow I managed to get to the other side even when I thought it wasn't possible . . . It took a while to get there, but I'm here. I want my relationship with food to help other girls and women, and my younger sister Eloise. She was a main driving force because I wanted to protect her so badly from what I went through.

And I never want YOU to feel stuck the way I used to. That's why I do what I do, and it's also given me this freedom to be ME, all because of some of the decisions I made along the way . . . More on that later. :)

♡ *Olivia says:*
Health looks different on EVERYONE 🙌 and if anyone is reading this and struggling, I love you so much, and this world is so much better with who you authentically are in it. 🤍 🩹

## Three Lil Things

### *It started with a lil freckle!*

Learning to accept myself, find comfort and be OK with how I look and who I am has been a big journey. **What do you like about yourself?** I don't know about you, but I think that's one of the hardest questions anyone can ask! When I was in recovery from anorexia, my therapist asked me this question and, sadly, at the time, I didn't think that I liked ANYTHING about myself.

I had to think for aaaages about something I liked. I know it sounds really strange, but I remember the first thing that I ever decided I was going to like about myself was . . . a tiny lil freckle on my pinky finger. I liked the placement of it; I thought it was elegant. Ha!

That lil freckle was the gateway to very slowly starting to like other things about myself. I gradually realised that there were other lil things that I liked about myself – including my hair and my newly found soft skin, now that I was in recovery.

You're probably wondering how all this can help you, especially if you're feeling a bit unlovable right now. :(

Honestly, you don't have to love everything about yourself. But even on days when you're feeling rubbish, you can find three lil things that you like about yourself.

For me, it started off with a lil freckle . . .

✦ Now, just to explain, it's **NOT** about getting up each morning and staring at yourself in the mirror and working out what you like and what you don't like. That is **NOT** what I'm asking you to do.

✦ This is not a daily challenge either, but every now and then it's nice to think about what you've got rather than worrying about what you don't have. Focus on lil things you like and tell yourself, 'I've got great boobs,' rather than, 'Oh, I've got this lump and roll here . . .'

✦ You might think of three different lil things each time. One day, it might be your skin, your kindness and your sense of humour. Another day it might be your smile, your excitable nature and your squishy belly!

✦ **Whatever they are, just think of the three lil things you like about yourself and I promise you, you'll feel a bit happier once you've listed those three lil things in your head.**

## Olivia says:

Try just choosing three things at a time. They can be anything – literally the first few things that come to mind 🧠 . . .

For instance, here's my lil list of three things:

- I'm soft and cuddly ☁
- I like my wobbly bits 🤓
- I love my nurturing side 🫶

So, next time you compare yourself to someone else or focus on the things you don't have, remember the bits you do have.

91

# Section 2: ✦ Changing Attitudes ✦

## Nobody is perfect

*It's the lil things that make us extra lovable* ✦

Your body type is not new and, once upon a time, it was actually seen as ideal. This is because beauty standards are **CONSTANTLY** evolving.

The way your body looks is due to all your ancestors (the people who came before you in the last decades and centuries) who loved each other and saw some of the traits you now have as beautiful.

The truth is that nobody is perfect. Nobody! In fact, there's no such thing as 'perfect' when it comes to the way we look. Every single person has 'flaws' and quirks which make them who they are. You're no different and neither am I. :)

It's those lil things that make us extra lovable – not always to ourselves but to our loved ones. Think about someone you love so much and how their lil differences that make them unique make them so . . . them.

But when we're surrounded by images of 'perfect' looking people on TV, in magazines and online, who all fit a very narrow image, it can be hard not to judge ourselves against those images.

I want to show you how the concept of the 'ideal body' has changed over the years up to where we are now, in today's world of social media, celebrities, diet culture, photo editing and filters. I hope that maybe you will be able to see how crazy it all really is. And maybe, just maybe, you'll see that nothing about you is ever truly wrong.

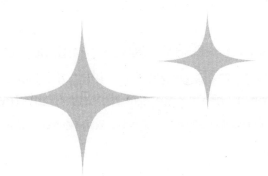

## Your body type is not new

*Understanding changing body trends and beauty standards*

Every time I'm having a bad body image day, my absolute favourite thing is to remind myself of the lessons that I used to have at college when I did history of art for A level . . . no, stop, I know this sounds boring, but bear with me!

So, in those lessons, I learned all about the artists of the Renaissance era.

**Renaissance:** A period in European history a LONG time ago, between 1300 and 1500, when there were huge advances in art, sculpture, philosophy, language, writing and science.

During this time, it was **BEAUTIFUL** to have cellulite and lil lumps and bumps and curves – totally different to what toxic diet culture portrays as 'beautiful' today. They would paint women and exaggerate their lil dimples and their softness. Check out some Renaissance art on your phone if you don't believe me.

You don't have to be into history or art to see that those Renaissance women's bodies look no different to a lot of the women you see walking around in their bikinis on the beach today.

**Curves were THE beauty standard back then. When I look at those paintings of naked Renaissance women now, I just think they're so beautiful – and they WERE seen as beautiful back then.**

So, whatever your body shape, never forget that your body type is not new; it's been around for longer than you can even imagine. It may not be the one trending at this moment in time, and for that, I am truly sorry, but that just proves how weird it is that bodies can even be trends. 😺

**Let's think about other body trends through history:**

✦ One of the earliest examples of art, dating to around thirty thousand years ago, is the Venus of Willendorf, a statue of a woman featuring big ol' boobs, hips and tummy.

500 BCE ✦ Ancient Greek statues, from around 500 BCE, also depict curvy women with lil rolls.

1480 ✦ The Renaissance era celebrated curves in works such as 'The Birth of Venus', painted by Italian artist Sandro Botticelli in the mid-1480s.

**1630** ✦ Peter Paul Rubens painted 'The Three Graces' in the 1630s, depicting three goddesses frolicking in the woods. They had cellulite, back fat and rolls and were **GODDESSES** – a vision of perfect beauty at the time.

**1837** ✦ During the Victorian era (1837–1901), women's bellies were painted to be a lil extra round, and that curve was celebrated – it was seen as a sign of fertility and femininity. Victorian women accentuated their curves with restrictive undergarments, and some women even wore corsets during pregnancy. They also used poisonous make-up to make their skin look paler, which was a trend at the time.

**1920** ✦ In the 'roaring' 1920s, the
flapper girl trend brought
about a revolution in fashion
and the ideal body type.
Curves were officially out
of fashion, and undergarments
were used to reduce bust size.
More people got bathroom
scales in their homes,
fuelling society's obsession
with body weight . . .

**1950** ✦ During the 1950s and 1960s,
the world fell in love with
Hollywood bombshells like
Marilyn Monroe – and curves
were back in fashion, with
an hourglass shape the most
sought after.

1960 ✦ **In the late 1960s, it was back to skinny, with Swinging Sixties superstar Twiggy being held as the feminine ideal. Being stick thin with long limbs was the ideal body type.**

1980 ✦ **By the 1980s, it was the supermodel era when tall, athletic models such as Cindy Crawford and Naomi Campbell were all the rage. Being tall and thin was seen as the 'perfect' figure.**

1990 ✦ **In the 1990s, supermodel Kate Moss was shorter, at only 1.7 m, but thin was still very much in. This was when extremely thin and androgynous (looking neither masculine or feminine) was ideal, and the number of people suffering from eating disorders began to increase dramatically worldwide.**

**2000** ✦ **By the 2000s, skinny was still the thing, but boob jobs were more popular, for getting back the curves lost due to weight loss. Cosmetic surgery was starting to become more prevalent.**

**Today** ✦ **Do we see a theme going on here . . . the constant changes? These days, I'm sure you're aware of the pressures for girls and women to look a certain way. Beauty standards are forever changing and will inevitably change in our lifetime, depending on celebrities and the media and so on.**

So, do you see now how beauty standards are only ever temporary ideals? Maybe you don't feel like you fit in today's current 'ideals', but you would have at some point in time . . . 10,000%.

**EVERY SINGLE** body type has at one point been a trend and has been sought after and seen as the most beautiful. **EVERY SINGLE BODY TYPE.**

Whenever you feel like you're not living up to these mythical ideals, remind yourself that even if you did achieve today's 'look', the standards will soon change. You know what won't change? How beautifully, uniquely **YOU** you are.

# Don't believe everything you see!!

## Some online images aren't telling the whole truth

I've shown you how, throughout history, standards of beauty have been depicted through paintings and sculptures. These days, photo editing apps and filters can have the same effect . . .

What I'm saying is, just because someone looks amazing in a photo online, it doesn't mean that it hasn't been edited. There's every chance that the images and videos you're seeing online aren't telling the whole truth at all.

Here are my lil tips for seeing through this:

✦ **Firstly, remember that social media is not real and influencers are a very small percentage of people who choose to put themselves online – it's basically their job!**

✦ Don't fall into the trap of believing the 'perfect' online image. They're just human beings like you and me; not the flawless 2D image you see on a screen.

✦ Remember that you're only seeing their very best bits because that's what they're showing you. Just like when you post your best picture online, out of a whole reel of pics . . . it's a natural instinct to want to show up as your best. And this is OK, but somewhere along the lines, things can start to get a lil out of hand.

✦ If you saw these people in real life, you'd see their other bits that perhaps they don't show online – like a squishy lil belly or a lil small bum. But maybe they choose not to show them on social

media. And that's perfectly **OK** too  –
we can't expect everyone to share
their deepest insecurities with us. ☺

✦ You can hide things online – and this
goes back to the point about nobody
being perfect. Everyone has a lil hang-
up. Some people might even have
surgery to try to fix the bits they're
insecure about – what you're seeing
might not be real.

✦ Posing can make someone look
completely different – perhaps they
have a 'best side' (I think I definitely
do 🤓) or always pose in certain
positions. Loads of influencers – and
celebrities too – learn how to pose for
photos to look their absolute best. All
the bad pics get deleted (I think we all
know this, though)!

✦ Then there's lighting, which actually makes a bigger difference than you might realise . . . It can make you look super smooth or add texture or change the colour of your skin.

✦ When you look at an influencer's pic or vid, you're seeing a split-second moment which sometimes has taken aaaages to create. It's not the same as when you take a selfie in your bedroom, so don't try to compare how you look to how an influencer looks.

✦ When you're scrolling online, you may not realise the cosmetic procedures someone has had.

✦ **Bear in mind that everything I've listed here comes together to create a smokescreen and an illusion of something that is unattainable and sometimes not actually real.**

✦ **And sometimes they're REALLY not real – AI influencers are a thing!**

So, I'll say it again: nobody has this perfect life. **NOBODY** . . . It doesn't exist!

# The dangers of online diet advice

## You can't trust everything that everyone says and does online

The truth is that if a diet you see online seems extreme and restrictive and designed to leave you feeling really hungry, then it's probably not healthy. Also, you should realise that this person may be a victim of diet culture themselves. Some influencers who talk about their 'healthy' diets may actually have issues with food and may even suffer from disordered eating or eating disorders themselves.

While I do occasionally share my lil 'what I eat in a day' vids online, I do so because I know I have a healthy relationship with food now and have learned a lot over the years. And when I was struggling, I always wanted to see what a 'normal' person would eat in a day (what even is 'normal'? But you get me). Anyway, I still don't claim to be an expert and never will . . . Leave that to the dietitians.

If you're not sure who someone is online or what qualifications they have to talk about food and nutrition, then always be very careful! If you have a question about healthy eating, the best thing to do is get trusted information from a website like nhs.uk or from qualified experts such as registered dietitians who are focused on health and balance and not restrictive dieting.

**FROM CHRISTINA, OUR DIETITIAN:**
We often want quick results, but diet promises just don't deliver. Instead, we are harming our health and wellbeing in the long run.

# Staying safe online

## Tips for looking after yourself in a digital world

Listen, I love social media and my lil corner of the internet. It feels like a lil safe space for me and hopefully for my followers too. But there is another side to the internet – a side it's important for you to be aware of. Here are some things to remember:

✦ **Anyone can see what you post depending on your privacy settings and this even means your parents if they want to . . . Seriously, I had friends share stuff about me, and my parents found it and I was in SO MUCH trouble!**

- ✦ Trolls are basically online bullies – they might even be mean under a comment you leave, so sometimes just be a lil careful.

- ✦ You might post something online that you later regret (and upset your friends or other people in the process too).

- ✦ Sometimes, people will try to trick you into clicking dangerous links or sharing things about yourself, such as pics of yourself that should really stay private.

- ✦ Be careful of catfishing, which is when a person pretends to be someone online but is actually someone completely different IRL.

✦ **If you arrange to meet up with someone who you've only chatted with online, you may only realise once you're face to face with them that they are not who they seemed.**

Here are a few of my lil tips to staying **safe** and **happy** online:

✦ **NEVER arrange to meet up with someone you only know online.**

✦ **If someone is asking you for personal details, such as where you live or where you go to school, RED FLAG ⚑ – go tell someone you can trust, parents or caregivers, or a teacher.**

- **If someone is trying to persuade you to do something you're not comfortable with – like posting a naked selfie or sending a nasty message to someone else, follow your instincts and DON'T do it.**

- **Think about how the posts you make now might still be around in decades, even if you delete them. It only takes seconds for someone else to screenshot a post or pic and send it on. TRUST ME. ☻ If you're at a party and having a lil too much 'fun', make sure nobody is filming you. When I was thirteen, I was kissing a boy and someone secretly filmed me. The video ended up being seen**

by my brother and was sent to my parents
... One of the most mortifying and worst
experiences of my life EVER. If this happens
to you, tell your parents, caregivers or an
adult you trust to help you.

✦ Respect your friends on social media. Don't
post pics of them that they might find
embarrassing unless they've said that you
can – and take them down if they change
their mind.

✦ Be careful how you word things, because
posts might be read differently to how
you'd intended.

*Olivia says:*

**Having fun and wanting to do what ur friends are doing is understandable, but please learn from me. I'm not saying that u shouldn't have fun and be yourself, I'm just saying that u should keep some things between u and your friends. If it's online, anyone can find it, and yes, that means your school and parents. 😄 IT'S NOT WORTH IT!!!**

# Setting myself free

## Why I set up my TikTok account :)

I remember so clearly sitting my parents down one day in my room and saying: 'Guys, I want to put my rolls on the internet . . . Is that OK?'

They were very confused. 😅

Maybe it was a strange thing to ask, but here's why . . .

When I was struggling with my eating disorder, my whole life revolved around not eating and then the side effects of that. I didn't talk to anyone for months, aside from my family. I didn't even speak to my closest friends.

Once I was finally in recovery, in early summer 2020, I started to realise that I'd spent all my teenage years trying to hide my insecurities, and I was exhausted with living like that.

I'd starved myself, spent hours researching every calorie under the sun, spent years trying different diets, only for it all to end in a big ol' eating disorder. Now I was in recovery, and gaining back the weight I'd lost, I decided that I wanted a different life for myself.

## I was DONE hiding.

**But the truth was that while I wanted so much to be free from diets and calorie counting and all the misery that went along with that, I was also really nervous about people seeing me again now that I'd gained some weight.**

I knew first-hand the dangers of following 'healthy diets' from online influencers, so I knew there was a LOT of misinformation out there. What I had learned from my dietitians honestly helped me so much, and my feed was full of toxic diet culture and I wanted to be a lil change for good. So I had an idea. I was going to post online about my recovery from an eating disorder and about how my body actually looks – not just when it's posed, but the parts I felt I had to hide my whole life. I'd always been so afraid of letting people see the real me, but now I felt like putting myself out there. I wanted to set myself free.

**My parents got used to the idea and so, two days after I'd explained it to them, on 21 July 2020, I posted my very first TikTok video:**

*'This is what I eat in a day in anorexia recovery.'*

It was, like, a lil food diary video. I was still on strict meal plans from my dietitians and showed what I ate through the day, including yoghurt and granola followed by a banana and a pear for breakfast, a tuna and cream cheese bagel with vegetables for lunch and chocolate for a snack. I even went out for dinner with my best friend – my first meal out since my eating disorder treatment. I ordered pasta with broccoli on the side and it felt like a **BIG** moment. 😳

I was trying to show that you can eat a normal day's food, partly to help me focus on my recovery but also to help other girls like me. I was getting professional help that I knew not everyone else could get and I wanted to share it. I grew up being told how horrible the internet was, and while I definitely still agree with this at times 😅, I found the comments I was getting from complete strangers at the time the kindest words ever. I was sort of taken aback by how lovely people were being and how supportive they were.

The next day, I posted another video – a close-up of me doing my make-up, with a bit about my story:

*'I lost a year of my life to anorexia. I stopped going out and talking to my friends. I lost my period, my hair, but mainly myself. The fear of people's judgement held me back so much. It just started as another diet. But I became obsessed with the numbers, colours and textures of food. I never thought it would be me who would develop an eating disorder. Choosing recovery is the best choice I've ever made. I chose recovery for myself, my younger sister, my friends and my future children. I've been on such a journey of disordered eating for many years and have so much I want to share. No one deserves to be uncomfortable in their own skin.'*

**The comments were so supportive . . . It was the first time that I'd had comments from people about my story helping them, and it made me feel so proud and kept me focused on my recovery. Getting such a positive reaction motivated me to post more.**

The thing is, though, that something inside me had changed as I was making and posting those first few vids. All my life, I'd cared SO much what other people thought of me. But now I finally came to the realisation that it didn't matter what other people thought of me – what mattered was that I was posting these videos because it was something I wanted to do and it was important to **ME.**

In September 2020, I went to uni and was a lil too busy to post much on TikTok. Not long after I'd started my second first year at uni (yes, my studies were really going that badly after I failed my first year exams 🐼), I decided not to continue my course. Deep down, it had always been my dream to become a midwife, and I planned to start my training the following year. I even did a work placement at a GP practice, which I loved.

So I left uni and moved back home to live with my family and, with more time to make videos, I posted more on TikTok. By this time, I'd gained weight and had reached what I now know is my set point weight – a healthy weight range which my body is able to maintain thanks to a balanced diet.

The more that I posted about myself and my body on TikTok, the more comfortable I felt in my own skin. I had more curves and lil rolls and I was OK with that because I knew that I was healthy, even if I didn't have a flat stomach. I was soft and cuddly and I'd more than accepted this – **I'd embraced it!**

Posting on TikTok had always just been a lil hobby for me, but by February 2022, my posts were getting loads more likes and views, and I was like, 'Hang on a minute, I could actually do this as a career!' I decided I would go back to university to do midwifery in a few years, when I was older. But for now, I wanted to be an online content creator, spreading my message and making my fun lil videos.

Honestly, I never ever in a million years thought that I'd get so much support . . . Never in a trillion years. And I never realised it would carry on for so long. For me, sharing my lil vids and pics online meant that, for the first time in my life, I didn't feel alone. 📖

OK, so now and then I got the odd nasty comment – random people saying that I looked pregnant or that I was ugly. Usually trolls have quite descriptive ways of saying this . . . Whatever! 😁 But, honestly, I knew that if these people met me in real life, they would actually probably be lovely to me (lol) and, in my mind, I told them to get well soon 😊 (for more tips on dealing with trolls and criticism, go to my Life Lesson 'Get well soon' on page 149). Anyway, the supportive, positive comments were what mattered, and they made me feel so happy and proud.

**Now I can be that person that I always needed growing up. The truth is that if all social media got deleted tomorrow, I genuinely wouldn't care, because having my TikTok account – and building an amazing, supportive community – has already changed me**

forever. It helps me stay on track with my recovery and it makes me braver too. Some of the things that I've been able to do, thanks to my social media platform, have been totally out of my comfort zone. It's been like exposure therapy.

**FROM MAYVRILL, OUR COUNSELLOR:**
Exposure therapy is a psychological treatment which helps people confront their fears by facing them rather than avoiding them. Along with the use of other therapies, such as CBT, a person can be gently guided to let go of self-sabotaging scripts and to choose to accept their body's uniqueness.

*Olivia says:*

**Just FYI, setting urself free doesn't mean having to not care about the way you look. I still love every girly thing there is: make-up, fashion, hairstyles — all of it! What I mean by setting urself free is no longer hiding ur true self or sacrificing your health by constantly trying to change parts about u that can't be changed. :)**

And now I'm writing this book and sharing my story with you . . . A total dream come true! I'm just so thankful for all these opportunities that have come my way. So now you can see how I set myself free – and I hope that, if you feel the same way as I used to do, you can find your own way to set yourself free too. And I'll be right here for you every step of the way.

## Olivia says:

**I'm so grateful for how far I've come 🌅 and I truly couldn't have done it without u guys. 🫶 🩹 I find it very fulfilling. I love what I do. Not only do I have an amazing community, but for the first time in my life, I feel like I've got a purpose. I'm doing something. I'm helping people, and I can be there for u all the way that I needed growing up.**

## My Cute Lil Formula

*Follow my formula for self-acceptance*

Whether it's your lil rolls or your stretchies or your lil double chin or whatever . . . I fully get how it feels when you can't stop thinking about your 'flaws', and I do it too, sometimes, when I'm having a 'bad body image' day. But there's a lil thing I like to do that I started accidentally, and I very soon realised how much it actually helped me . . . My Cute Lil Formula!

**It's really easy. All you have to do is stick 'my cute lil' in front of (any insecurity you have).**

So, to help myself accept my belly rolls, I started talking about 'my cute lil belly' and then it went on to 'my cute lil soft dimples' (cellulite . . . hahaha), and 'my cutie lil bump on my nose' (it's something only I see). It could be your cute lil ponytail or literally anything in the worlddd. I even use it to describe things I love and it just makes everything sound better. ☺ Instead of going, 'Ughhhh, my belly,' it's, 'My cute lil belly', and it doesn't matter how you say it.

It made me realise that saying something was 'cute' made it easier to accept it, and since then, I've been doing it in all my videos. And there's just something about the word 'lil' . . . It makes you smile. Think about it – cute lil chubby babies are so cuddly and adorable. Seriously, having a bit of squishiness or a roll here and there is natural. When you see a baby elephant, you're going to call it cute, right? It's a cute lil elephant. OK, so it's not a tiny thing, but it's still cute – and cute doesn't have to be about size and being all teeny weeny and ickle. Like, a baby elephant could probs crush me, but it's still the cutest thing ever.

**Some people might suggest that you try boosting your self-confidence by looking in the mirror and calling yourself beautiful but, tbh, that's never worked for me and has never once made me feel better. My brain just can't believe it sometimes, and I'm left feeling worse.**

Staring at yourself in the mirror and telling yourself that you're beautiful doesn't evoke those fuzzy warm feelings (for me) . . . but calling yourself cute does, I find, because it's just so much easier to accept – like, yes, I am in fact a cutie pie. 🐷 I don't care if you think I'm uggers; you can't deny that I'm adorable even when I look my worst – when I have the flu or something, I just look like a cute lil ill person.

*Olivia says:*

**At the end of the day, it's speaking kindly to urself that makes a difference; however, when u feel awful, it's so, so hard to do!! So try my #cutelilformula next time!! U don't have to 'love it' – u just have to acknowledge that it is also actually just very cute.**

## Be the change

### *Hype others*

Have you ever given someone a compliment and seen how their face lights up and then you get all happy and excited too? But then maybe in another situation, when you're stuck in a moment of comparison instead, you feel a lil jealous or bad about yourself?

You see, comparison IS the thief of joy. There's nothing wrong with you if you find yourself stuck feeling this way, but it doesn't feel nice . . .

So try complimenting someone instead. It can help shift you into appreciating them and spark a lil moment of happiness, and you might even make a new friend.

When you compare yourself to other people, you can go down two avenues. Feeling jealous is one path you could take and, let's face it, everyone feels jealous sometimes. But jealousy isn't a nice emotion and it will never make you happy in yourself — and, well, it's isolating too.

The other path you could take is much nicer . . .
Let me explain.

I'm the sort of person who LOVES to hype people
up . . . It's just what I like to do. When I meet you for
the first time, I will usually compliment you on something!
And do you know what? It makes me so happy to know
that by complimenting someone else, I've made them feel
good. And I think it's made me learn to see the good in
people too. In my mind, I see something I like and I blurt
it out, and not once has it led to a bad encounter.

♡ *Olivia says:*

**Giving compliments is a win-win situation.**
**The other person gets a confidence boost**
**and u feel like ur a rlly good person . . .**
**because u are. ;)**

By hyping up others, it stops you from falling into the trap of comparing yourself to them. You just can't – the two things don't exist together. Honestly . . . try it!

Also, while you should never give to receive, you know what? You might get a little confidence-boosting compliment back your way in return! So it starts off this little chain of warm fuzzy feelings and kindness and loveliness . . . It is the BEST. I'm not saying that you should necessarily be commenting on their bodies – that might feel a bit too personal – but I'm hugely clothes and beauty orientated (you might have noticed . . . haha) so I'll say something like:

💜 **'OMG, your hair colour is stunning!'**

💜 **'What lip gloss are you wearing, because it looks amazing on you?'**

💜 **'Where did you get those jeans, because they look so good on you and I need them!'**

If you feel a bit shy and weird about it at first, I get that. Trust me, although I come across as loud and bubbly, I can still be a very anxious person, especially when I'm meeting new people — but I find that giving compliments is a great ice breaker and really helps me overcome my nervousness.

Just think — by hyping other people, whether it's your friends, your family or even someone you've just met, you can set in motion this lil wave of happiness. Because if other people see you being kind and positive, maybe they'll go off and give out compliments and make other people feel good about themselves too.

*Olivia says:*

**If everyone did this, we'd all feel so much more secure and self-confident, wouldn't we? We could literally BE THE CHANGE we all need and spread good feelings everywhere we go.**

# Section 3:
## ✦ My 10 Life Lessons ✦

These are the things I wish I'd known when I was growing up, and some have taken me yearsss to realise. From dealing with not feeling good enough to finding enough confidence to take cute pics with your friends. And now I'm going to share them with you . . . Yay!

## 1. Your ✧ESSENCE✧

### *What makes you YOU*

You are more than what you look like — and I'm sure you've heard this before. But what I mean is you have special lil things about you that make you funny, or interesting, or caring . . . You get the picture.

It's like when you meet someone who has so much charm or just something ✧special✧ about them and you find yourself super drawn to them . . . That's their essence.

It's the things that make us likeable or different. Sometimes it's hard to figure out exactly what your own essence is, but we all have it, and everyone's essence is unique.

## It's what makes you ✦YOU✦.

When you're feeling low about yourself, it's easy to forget that you have more to offer other people than just how you look. Try to remember that even when someone looks like the most gorgeous human, that doesn't automatically make them an amazing person, right? It's about who we are as people.

If I'm having a bad body image day, I'll try to focus instead on who I want to be and what I like about myself as an actual person ... My ✦essence✦.

I love to think of myself as nurturing and caring, and that my personality is a big ol' warm hug . . . Familiar and friendly. I'm bubbly and excitable and make things more fun sometimes just by being me. And no one can tell me otherwise, because these are things I already think about myself.

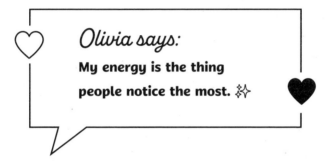

Olivia says:

**My energy is the thing people notice the most.** 🌠

When I was really ill with anorexia, I completely lost myself, my personality and my essence – it was completely zapped away. I lost sight of the things I liked about myself and my dreams. During my treatment, on hard days, it helped me to remember *why* I wanted to get better and that my body had a function that was important to me, which was to hopefully have children one day. Right now, my purpose is to help other people not to go down the path I did. I guess that's part of my essence too, which is something I'm proud to say. :)

So what's your essence?

✦ **Try to think about the things you like about yourself.**

✦ **It could be how in tune with music you are, how engaging you are to talk to or that you give the best advice, or it could be that you're funny, or thoughtful, or full of energy, or creative . . .**

✦ **Finding your essence is just about identifying the things that make you a lil different or special, and it's all up to you. :)**

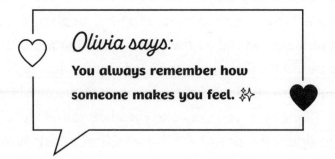

*Olivia says:*
**You always remember how someone makes you feel.** ✧

# 2. Your cuddly bits

## *Portable human pillow*

Growing up, I assumed that I would have a flat stomach like girls I saw in magazines and online, and I hated my squish. It was only after recovering from anorexia that my feelings slowly shifted. I realised that I gave the best cuddles. I loved how soft my skin was now that I was eating enough. I also realised that, by always focusing on my appearance, I hadn't appreciated how great my body was in other ways.

*Olivia says:*

**My legs let me walk and run, my belly digests food to give me energy, my arms let me hug people I love, my hands let me text my friends, my eyes let me see the sky and sunset, my mouth lets me experience the flavour of yummy foods, and I don't have to think about any of it . . . My body does it all for me.**

During my recovery, I'd worried about what a future boyfriend might think of my squishy bits. Silly, I know, but it's the truth. I came to the conclusion that my soft belly felt just like my boobs and that, if someone liked me, they'd be fine with ALL my squishy bits. If someone only liked my lumps of fat in specific places, then they weren't for me. And the same applies to you too, whatever your body shape, whether you're slim or curvier.

I know now that my own natural body shape doesn't come with a flat stomach, and I love my lil curves and being soft and cuddly. Accepting and embracing my squishy side is something I post about online. I love showing my cute lil belly to help other girls realise that their bellies are normal and cute too. The best thing ever is when my followers and friends say they've accepted their wobbly bits. :))))

When I think of my body, I find it helps to come up with lil analogies and sayings . . .

- ✦ 'I'm like a portable human pillow.'

- ✦ 'I am as soft and fluffy as a cloud . . .
  I too have lil lumps and bumps and curves.
  I'm not as smooth as glass . . . I'm as soft
  and as snuggly as a cloud. ☁️✨'

- ✦ 'Just because a sunset is beautiful doesn't
  make a flower any less gorgeous too. ☺️'

- ✦ 'Not every day is easy 🤍 but it's so, so
  much better than waking up afraid you
  have gained weight, than waking up and
  feeling hungry and not allowing yourself
  to eat, than constantly checking how flat
  your stomach is. So, so much better.'

- ✦ 'Health looks different on EVERYONE.'

- ✦ 'Honestly, when u lie down and ur belly
  flops, omg SO CUTEEEE. When it's a lil
  squishy . . . I think it's adorable.'

## Olivia says:

Being cuddly, for me, is just what my body looks like when it's working at its optimum. We all look different and, just remember, only a very teeny tiny percentage of people actually have the figure of a straight-size model. ♡ It's not safe to make ur body look a certain size if that's not what ur body is supposed to look like. I tried for many years, thinking that's just what I had to do. Being skinny never brought me the happiness – being healthy has. ♡

## 3. You don't have to love everything about yourself — but you can like it

*It's OK to learn to like the lil bits that you're uncomfortable with*

First up, I want to say that I'm not always happy with how I look, and do you know what? That's normal and OK. You might not love every inch of your body, but you can learn to be OK with some bits — and maybe even like them.

When I was struggling with my eating disorder and with body dysmorphic disorder, I had constant intrusive thoughts, about my face, my hairline, my thighs . . . A never-ending list.

**FROM MAYVRILL, OUR COUNSELLOR:**
Around 90% of the population experience intrusive thoughts. Having intrusive thoughts is when you experience distressing, senseless, unwanted thoughts, images or urges that suddenly appear in your mind. Because the way we think affects the way we feel, these emotions can then affect our actions or reactions. With support, therapy can help someone to become aware of how they can change the thoughts and behaviours which are creating negative outcomes in their lives. Talk to your GP, parents or caregivers if this is something you need support with.

I was SO obsessed with fixing these things, I would stand in front of the mirror and stare at myself for hooourrs and feel so incredibly miserable.

Constantly obsessing over specific features isn't healthy for your state of mind. If you're falling into a cycle of negative body checking, here are my tips:

✦ **Remember that in real life, nobody will focus on one lil detail about you. When other people look at you, your body won't be in one fixed stance – you'll look different with every angle and expression.**

✦ **See yourself as a whole instead of honing in on details. I used to wear layers of white concealer on my undereye bags and I realise now that it didn't suit me at all! I didn't see it at the time because I was so focused on that specific feature. Now, I only use a tiny dab of concealer because I see my face and body as a whole and don't obsess over that small detail.**

## ✦ It's OK to pose nicely in the mirror and put on clothes that make you feel good because it's healthy to see yourself in a positive light.

Now, here's another thing – and this is my main point – you don't have to LOVE yourself in your 'rawest form' (just out of bed, with unwashed hair and wearing spot cream). There is no rule book saying that you have to look your best every second of the day. I don't know if I'll ever totally love myself in my rawest form, but I've learned to accept that this is just how I look in that one moment, and then I carry on my day without stressing.

These days, I even leave the house without putting on make-up or doing my hair. It doesn't mean that I don't still love make-up and love to get all glam, because I do, a hundred per cent. But I also get to just relax and exist as a greasy potato too. ☺

Do you know what also helps? Noticing the bits about me that I DO like! So I might tell myself, 'OK, well I love my boobs . . . They're not perfect, but I'm just gonna enjoy the fact that I like them and focus on the reasons why I do.'

Whenever you hear a mean voice in your head, focus on what you think is cute or even just OK about yourself, and the rest will come naturally.

## 4. Everyone has a thing they don't like

*Everyone – you just don't see it because people hide their insecurities*

You might look at other girls and think that they look perfect, but you know what? Underneath their clothes, they just have a body like you . . . They have a vagina, boobs, areolas, body hair and scars.

In recovery, I remember my psychiatrist told me to go to a nudist beach one day if I could. I was like, *Okayyy.* 😁 But once I was in my twenties, during summer 2023, I actually did – and it made sense! When people are naked and not posing, with no make-up, no clothes perfectly positioned or fancy bikinis, and instead they're simply ✨**existing**✨, they are just . . . bodies. I've also done a life drawing class (no, I wasn't the model!) and it felt the same – **just a body.**

**Everyone feels self-conscious about something and, let's face it, most of us (including me) try to hide our insecurities from the outside world. At some point, everyone feels that they're lacking something – or have too much of something.**

Maybe you'll wear certain clothes to hide those insecurities, or do your make-up or hair a specific way. All through my teens, people thought that I had big ol' boobs because I alwayssss would wear a push-up bra! Because I hid my insecurities, nobody knew that at that time I felt I was lacking. Now my body type has changed, and as my boobs have filled out, so have other parts, and that could lead to new insecurities. It's a never-ending cycle.

*Olivia says:*
**That perfect version of urself in your head is impossible to achieve because u will never have it ALL. No one does . . . Even if u think they do, I promise they don't. Everyone has their insecurities.**

I meet the most gorgeous humans in the world because of my job as an influencer, and when they tell me their own insecurities, I'm always surprised, cause I NEVER would have guessed!

**You can never REALLY know exactly what's going on with someone's life or inside their head. So it's about understanding that nobody has the perfect life or the perfect body and that's just reality – it's LIFE.**

And most people would tell you that, too, once you get to know them. It's just they can't possibly put a daily reminder on social media or constantly share their deepest vulnerabilities. So it's our responsibility to keep this in mind. 📖

## 5. 'Get well soon'

*Dealing with comments*

Sometimes, it feels like everyone has an opinion about you. 'Oh, you've gotten bigger . . .' or 'You look different . . .' It's natural for people to be extra interested during a period of time when your body is changing so much, and they may very well have good intentions when doing this, but sometimes it's not appropriate. The annoying fact is that you're going to have to deal with insensitive comments at some point, because often people don't think before they speak!

The other thing is that people love to give advice – even when you haven't asked for it. If they notice that you've gained a lil weight or that you have lil bumpies on your face, they may want to advise you on your 'diet' or give you a lesson in skincare (aarggh!).

Before I developed my eating disorder, when my body was changing and going through all the normal fluctuations, adults close to me kept suggesting that I go to the gym or try running. Those sorts of insensitive comments can hurt, even if they come from a good place. As an insecure teenager, all you're going to hear when someone makes a comment like that is: 'There's something wrong with me and I need to change . . .'

**Then there are comments you might get online. Perhaps you've posted a pic and someone's made a negative comment which has left you feeling awful.**

So how do you deal with all this? Well, if something someone says hurts your feelings, they don't get to decide it doesn't hurt. They may have had no bad intentions, but it can still hurt, and that's OK and valid.

Being perfect and getting it right all the time is impossible. We will all mess up at some point and that's fine – we are ✨human✨. We can apologise and try to move on.

However, when it's intentional, then it's a different story.

No truly happy person is gonna be mean. This is the truth. If someone is happy with themselves, they won't feel the need to put you down. End of. Often, nasty comments stem from deep-rooted issues that THEY have, or possibly from envy, maybe because that person has noticed something in you that they wish they had.

In this situation, there's a lil saying you may have already heard:

## Jealousy is a disease . . .

So, in your mind, simply wish this jealous person well. Or, if you're feeling super brave, you could tell them to 'get well soon' . . . 👋🏃

## And then move on and don't give it another thought.

# 6. Friendships

## Your chosen family <3

Finding true friends, who have your best interests at heart, is a blessing. But the truth is that friendships can change, and friends come and go. It's hard when this happens, but it's part of life.

Sometimes, your friends are your friends because of convenience . . . Like being in the same class or doing the same activities. Perhaps they're your friends because you really click with them.

School can be a confusing whirlwind, and sometimes it sucks. No one wants to be left out, and there can be a lot of insecurity. Then there are the cliques – all the lil friendship groups. Every school is different, but one thing remains largely the same . . . the friendship group structures.

At secondary school, I longed to be 'accepted', and I think that's a common experience growing up. In Year 9, when I was thirteen, I found myself in the 'naughty group', shall we say. ;)

Even before I was in this group, I was constantly in trouble at school. But in this group, I found that I was more accepted because of my bad behaviour. Also, other people tried harder to be my friend because they liked the group that I was in.

However, trust me, being in 'that' sort of friendship group at school isn't quite like you'd think. Everyone assumes that those groups of people are super confident . . . but actually I found it was the opposite, and they didn't even really like each other, and a lot of it was fake and superficial.

It doesn't mean that, individually, those people aren't lovely, but within group situations, things can turn toxic. Eventually, after about a year, I came to my senses and I had a bust-up with the group, and other people who'd tried super hard to be my friend turned on me. If people only respect you because of who your friends are, that's a red flag.

And if someone has to use intimidation in order for you to respect them, then it probably comes from a place of their own insecurity and only holds as much power as you give them. Never forget that nobody is better than you and, also, that you're no better than anybody else. Once people grow up and recognise their silly behaviour for what it is, things usually change.

When I was older and in eating disorder recovery, after being a recluse for months, I was scared to go back out there and see friends again, but I finally realised, after years of never understanding, that **IT'S NOT ABOUT IF THEY LIKE ME; IT'S ABOUT IF I LIKE THEM.** Never forget that.

If you've ever felt what it's like to be left out by other people, you'll understand how horrible it is. But then, equally, when someone makes an effort with you, it's the best. At the end of the day, the friendships that are most fulfilling and fill you with confidence and security are with people who like you because of who you are – not how you look, who you know, how many followers you have on Instagram or who you've dated.

*Olivia says:*

**Being a caring person is gonna make other people respect u and want to be ur friend. Never underestimate how a small moment of kindness can make someone else feel.**

# 7. Looking after yourself

*Sometimes, the best person to look after you is . . . you*

We've all heard of self-care, but it can mean a lot of things. Basically, self-care is any activity or routine that helps you stay well – physically, mentally and emotionally. Here are a few self-care methods:

❤ **Maintaining your personal hygiene – brushing your teeth and keeping your face, hair and body clean**

❤ **Eating well and knowing the importance of a healthy balanced diet (for more info, go to pages 68–69)**

❤ **Getting enough sleep**

♥ Giving yourself time to relax doing things you love, such as watching your favourite TV shows, being creative or playing sport . . . Whatever fills your cup.

♥ Learning to say no to things you don't want to do or which you know would not be good for you

♥ You might feel your best when your routine includes movement you enjoy. This is about feeling good; it's **NOT** about changing your body! Whether you think the gym is like a playground with fun machines, or you want to dance in your bedroom, or get outside on a run – do whatever brings you joy

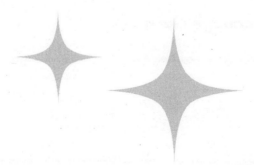

And here are some reasons why **self-care** is so important – it:

💙 **Supports your overall sense of wellbeing**

💙 **Helps boost your self-confidence and self-esteem**

💙 **Helps you understand who you are as a person and your needs**

💙 **Builds your resilience and ability to cope with life's challenges**

I know it can be hard to get on board with some self-care methods. You might not feel like having a shower every day or going to sleep at a decent hour. If you think of self-care as lil regular 'treats' you can give yourself, you may find it easier.

Here are ways you can be kind to yourself and your body:

✦ If it's your thing, wear underwear that makes you feel ✨good✨ – a bra, a crop top, some nice pants, a cute lil set . . . whatever feels good and makes you feel special.

✦ Put your favourite music on in your room and dance around like you're in a music vid on YouTube. It doesn't matter what you're wearing to do this – whether you're in your cute underwear or a pyjama set or your favourite dress or, in my case, straight out of the shower. 😄 All that matters is that you let loose and have fun.

✦ Make a 'feel good' playlist of songs that, well, make you feel good. ;) Mine would always include Selena Gomez and Taylor Swift. I'd stick on their songs and dance around my bedroom, imagining that I was in a music video. It always made me feel so good about myself . . . Try it!

✦ As well as dancing, try posing in front of the mirror for fun – I'm not talking about standing there staring at your reflection and pointing out all the things you don't like. Just dance and move and pose. It's fun and it helps you get to know your body more.

# 8. Hunger hormones

## Your relationship with food is sacred

After everything I've been through, I never thought it would be possible for me to have a healthy relationship with food. But thankfully now, even on bad body image days, I can still eat without going back into negative cycles.

**And if I can do it, so can YOU.**

During my eating disorder recovery, I learned how to eat a balanced diet and build a balanced plate of food, and it was a game changer!

**I'd grown up thinking that there were 'good' and 'bad' foods and that if I ate a donut and then fancied another, there was something wrong with me. :(**

But when I was in recovery, I came up with my 'cupcake analogy'. Have you ever seen a kid sucking on a cupcake wrapper? It's because they want another one. But maybe there are adults who won't let them have another one.

Perhaps you've done this yourself and there were adults who wouldn't let you have another cake either.

And so now you're older, you might feel guilty when you want another cupcake. But, really, it's natural to want more if something is yummy and you're hungry. And the more you tell yourself that you shouldn't have another cupcake, the more you're gonna think about it and maybe want one.

**However, if you allow yourself to see all food as 'neutral', where there is space for everything and nothing is 'forbidden', fun foods like cupcakes become less special because you no longer demonise them. After a while, you may even go through stages of not wanting a cupcake because you don't feel like it, as you know you can have it another time because you give yourself permission. This is a principle of intuitive eating.**

The dietitians who helped me in recovery taught me all about intuitive eating, which means listening and responding to your body when you're hungry and when you're full. It doesn't mean that if you want to eat donuts all day, that's what you're going to do! But it does mean that if you want a donut – or two – you can have it

. . . and that's more than OK. :) Over time, you might not crave donuts as much because you know you can have one if you want one. Intuitive eating still includes basic, healthy food rules.

**We need all the food groups in order to be healthy, and each food group has important benefits. Turn to pages 68–69 for a reminder!**

If you're following intuitive eating, it's really important that you know the basics of nutrition and how to eat a balanced diet and create a balanced plate of food.

**FROM CHRISTINA, OUR DIETITIAN:**
Intuitive eating is an approach to nutrition that encourages individuals to listen to their bodies and trust their internal cues when it comes to eating. The goal is to allow all types of foods, without guilt or judgement, removing the moral value attached to different foods. Just as it's important to respond to hunger cues, intuitive eating encourages individuals to recognise when they are comfortably full. It promotes body acceptance and respect for one's natural body shape and size – and it discourages the pursuit of unrealistic ideals promoted by diet culture.

When you're building up a balanced plate, whilst eating intuitively and listening to what your body really wants, ask yourself, 'What carbohydrate, protein, veg and fat am I craving?'

Then you can build your plate of food knowing that you're ticking all those boxes. It's good to have structure with food (at least that helped me), but being able to be flexible is also very important. Not every meal needs to be perfectly balanced – just try to eat an overall balanced diet – aim for 80% of your food being nutritious and 20% being fun!

*Olivia says:*

**If it feels like a constant fight to keep your body looking a certain way, or if feeding your body balanced meals makes you gain weight, maybe that's because the weight you are now is not the weight you're meant to be, and that's OK – because we all are meant to look different. We all have hair that grows different lengths, in different colours, in different curl patterns, just like how trees all have different branches. It's OK, and it's not a new thing. Somewhere along the line, looking different became wrong, but that's simply not true. It never was.**

## 9. How to get a cute photo

### 'For the memories'

Maybe you're camera shy, or maybe you hate how you look in photos? This used to be me too! Literally, I have barely any pictures of me from the age of fourteen to seventeen. :( Here's how I learned to get used to having my picture taken – now I actually find it so much fun!

✦ **Any time you take a picture, say 'it's for the memories', and this takes all the pressure off getting a good photo, because it's . . . for the memories, not to look good (bonus – now you have photos you can look back on – yay! Older you will be so happy, trust me).**

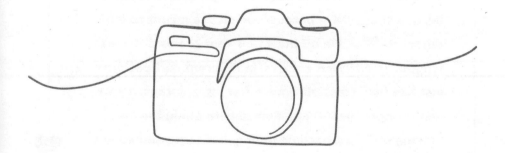

✦ When you're on your own at home, practise posing in the mirror or on your phone with the selfie timer, so that you can feel more confident and not like you don't know what you're doing when someone starts taking photos.

✦ Practise making your friends take photos of you just for 'the memories' . . . don't expect them to come out perfect, because they won't and it will take time to learn what you like. It will help you get used to it and become more confident to do your cute lil poses.

*Olivia says:*

With practice, u will hopefully start to get cute photos u like and u might even find it fun having lil photoshoots with ur friends. ☺

At some point, you're going to see a bad pic of yourself. Yes, I know it's rough and it makes you feel like you never want to leave the house again. But an unflattering photo isn't the end of the world. Think about it – every pic is just a split second of time. When you see a pic of someone else, it doesn't mean that's what they look like all the time, does it?

**Trust me, I've seen some horrendous pictures of myself – like, soooo bad. I remind myself that it's OK when someone has a picture of a sunset and says 'it doesn't do it justice' – it's the same with me.** 🤓

Also, you might look at that horrific pic in a few months and feel differently; you might even think it's actually hilarious or cute.

Once, I was lying on a sunbed on holiday and my dad took a pic of me with my lil rolls bulging over my bikini bottoms, double chin and starfishing. OMG, it was BAD. But I posted it online because it was funny. Everyone has that version of them.

Sometimes, someone – a friend or otherwise – might post an 'ugly' pic of you online. I've had that happen to me and it felt like they'd shown my worst insecurities to the world . . . Noo!

Here's how to cope if this happens to you:

✦ **If you're really uncomfortable with it, tell them to take it down – if they won't, that says more about them than about you, OK?**

✦ **Bear in mind that, while, yes, it's hurtful to you, no one else is going to pay much attention.**

✦ **If it's bearable, try to own it – tell yourself, 'Yes, that is a terrible pic, maybe even funny, but I don't look like that IRL.' This shows that you're confident in who you are and can see the funny side.**

✦ **Remind yourself that one pic isn't what you look like 24/7 and doesn't define you.**

*Olivia says:*

**Seen a bad photo of urself? Who cares! In real life these split seconds aren't what we see – it's not the 360 version of you, it's not your essence and it's not your ✨reality✨ – because, in real life, we don't walk around posed like we do in pics (could u imagine 😂). That pic of you at an angle you don't like? It's OK; you're not stuck like that. No one sees that split second of you frozen in time – for them, it's just a passing moment. 🫠💗**

# 10. Grateful noticing – ❋the lil things around you❋

## *Romanticise your environment*

Have you ever been to the beach and really paid attention to the grains of sand between your toes? Or watched raindrops fall down the window, or the sun shining through the branches of the trees, and thought, *Wow that's so amazing and prettyyyyyyy.*

This is a lil thing I do on days when things are overwhelming and I want to get out of my head and feel calmer and more ❋content❋. I call it 'grateful noticing' and it's essentially a form of mindfulness.

> **Mindfulness:** A therapeutic technique of being fully present in the moment, which means paying attention to your thoughts, feelings and bodily sensations. Practising mindfulness has been proven to boost mental health by reducing stress and improving your sense of wellbeing.

## By noticing things around you, it gives you something else to focus on, other than your feelings.

In recovery, I learned that 'grateful noticing' would help me in moments when I was struggling, and it was also a lil tool I used once I was feeling better. It's really easy and you can do it anywhere.

It's about noticing the smallest things, the tiniest details, around you – even just for one second – and being grateful for them. So you might be sitting in your room and you could look out of the window and think, *Oh, look at those bricks – there are orange ones and red ones and grey ones, and I like how all the different colours look together.* Trust me, you don't have to obsessively LOVE those bricks (haha). You just need to focus on them and appreciate them for a moment. When you're out in nature, it's super easy to do. You might notice a tiny leaf blowing in the wind, or there might be a cute lil squirrel darting about or some birds flying in the sky above you.

If it's one of those days when you feel too rubbish to even get out of bed (and believe me, I've had many of those days), you could focus on something more basic – like the fluff on your dressing gown or the pattern on your pyjamas.

**I know it may sound SO cringe, but it's a way of slowing down and breathing more easily again . . . and it really works, I promise you.**

*Olivia says:*

**You're not alone (even if it feels like it) and I'm sorry if u ever have these terrible days. I had them too and I'm still here. There is light at the end of that tunnel, I promise. Ur meant to be here, every part of u – I love u.** 🫶

# Mic Drop

## *A final word from Olivia*

Thank you for reading my book.

I hope that some of the things that I've said have resonated with you. I know how hard it can be on days when you feel beyond rubbish. Or maybe you don't have those days . . . and that's great! But if you do have those days, please know that there will be an end to them at some point in the future. We all find peace in life eventually, although it's a gradual thing.

**Growing up can be one of the hardest times in your life. Or it may be the best. Or maybe both. And it's OK to not be OK. It's OK to be struggling.**

**But you're not alone. You're loved. I love you, and there's a little spark inside you that needs to be here. You may not know it right now, but I promise that you will some day.**

When I was a teenager, I could never have imagined having the life that I have now. I never even thought that I would ever feel happy to be here. When I was feeling really low about myself, I could never see a way out of the misery . . . but, in the end, I found it. And if I can, so can YOU.

By reading this book, I hope you'll learn to:

💜 **Look at yourself and see some things you might like**

💜 **Accept your cuddly side**

💜 **Know that your ✨essence✨ is what really makes you memorable and what makes you . . . ✨you✨**

💜 **See how crazy the world is sometimes and understand that it's not your fault**

You might have thought that growing up to become a woman was all about make-up and handbags and looking pretty. And while I personally LOVE all of these things so much :)) becoming a woman is a big deal . . . It's a responsibility too. The world has come so far, but it's still not perfect. As women, we're the ones who have to look out for each other, to help one another when the rest of society places how we look above our wellbeing and the health of our bodies. 📖

Also, I want you to know that if you're ever struggling, I'm here for you and these words are for you. I hope you can pick this book up and know that I'm there beside you. The words in this book mean so much to me and they come from a deep place, and I hope that they can comfort you when you need them most.

*Love, Olivia xoxo*

# ✦ Acknowledgements ✦

I have so many people I want to say thank you to. The biggest thank you ever to my followers and anyone who has ever supported me; I will never forget my first TikTok I ever posted and all the sweetest comments from at the time complete strangers. 😊 You guys have shown me so much love, and it's truly melted my heart and continues to. 🫶🩹 Who would have thought that one lil video would eventually lead us here?!?!

None of this would be possible without my family – thank you for helping me through the crazy times and being there for me even when none of it made sense. To my mother, thank you for our late nights spent on the floor chatting. And to my father, thank you for letting me put my hair that was falling out on your bald head. 🫶🩹

To my sister: you have the most special place in my heart. I love you so extremely deeply, and no matter what life throws at us, you will always be my baby sister. The only thing that helped me open up at first was the thought that maybe I would be able to protect you from the same fate. I love you. I would do anything for you (almost 😊).

**181**

To my manager, Katie Ryan – without all your help, this wouldn't have been possible. You really are so amazing, and I admire every lil thought you have and appreciate your input always. 🐚

And the biggest thank you ever to Louise Baty: thank you for being so easy to talk to – you are totally the best!!!! 🦭

To my editors, Emily Lunn and Anna Martin, thank you so much for trusting me with this book. I admire you both so much, and to everyone in the Hachette team: Victoria Walsh, Emily Thomas, Bec Gillies, Jennifer Hudson, Lucy Clayton and Almaz Brooks. To my designers Samuel Perrett and Pippi Grantham-Wright, thank you for making this book so wonderfully pink. 🐷 This whole process has been completely alien to me, but you all have blown me away every step of the way. Thank you for your passion and care. 💜

I dedicated this book to my psychiatrist and dietitians in recovery and was so lucky to have Christina de Beukelaar on board with this project. Christina, thank you for teaching me and gifting me a healthy relationship with food. 🫶 It's truly changed my life and I wish the same now for everyone else. I can still remember all the lil stories you told me and hold them close to my heart and occasionally hear your voice in my head when I eat said specific foods. 🍽️ 🤓 Alexia Dempsey, you made me fall in love with dietitians; you guys are magic. 🫶 Thank you to Pippa Hembrey and special thank you to my psychiatrist in recovery, Dr Pippa Hugo – thank you so much for all your help. My kids will know your name. 😎

Thank you to Mayurill Freeston-Roberts for all your amazing insight, and thank you for being so supportive. 💟 Your words have really touched me.

And lastly, I want to say thank you to you – thank you for picking up this book. Here's to not allowing society's dieting obsession ruin our relationship with food and with our bodies. 🤝

Here's to our friends, our mothers, our future daughters and theirs too. Let's change it for all of us. 🫶

# Further reading and helpful information

If you need support or are looking for advice on some of the topics we've discussed, it's always best to speak to a trusted adult. You could also call your GP (or ask your parent or caregiver to do so) or speak to your school nurse. They will help you get the right treatment and support. And here are some other ways of getting the information you need:

**NHS Eat Well**

Read NHS guidance on eating a balanced diet here:
**www.nhs.uk/live-well/eat-well/**

**Beat**

An eating disorders charity that offers support for those with eating disorders and their families:
**www.beateatingdisorders.org.uk**

## Mind

A mental health charity supporting those with mental health problems: **https://www.mind.org.uk/**

## Young Minds

A mental health charity specifically for young people and teens: **www.youngminds.org.uk**

## Samaritans

A UK-based charity offering emotional support to people in distress. Whatever you're going through, you can call them any time, from any phone, for free on **116 123**, or email **jo@samaritans.org.** Find out more info on: **www.samaritans.org.**

# IF YOU LIKED THIS, WHY NOT TRY ...